MESSAGE

WITH

PURP**O**SE

Swipe Dating Simplified

MICHAEL BOOTHBY

Dedicated to single people everywhere.

CONTENTS

INTRODUCTION

"Most People Stink At Online Dating"
-Aziz Ansari, *Modern Romance*

"YOU'VE GOT A MATCH!"

Michael: Hey there! I noticed you just picked up "Message with Purpose: Swipe Dating Simplified" - I love your taste!

Reader: Hey Michael! Thanks! Yeah I did. I don't know much about it yet... I just picked it up.

Michael: Well I love that you're open-minded and willing to learn and grow. I'm always learning and growing myself.

Reader: I think so! What are you learning?

Michael: I'm learning how to write an introduction to a book. I saw in your profile that you love to read. Maybe we could get coffee this week, and you could help me out? :) I'm free Tuesday and Thursday afternoon.

Reader: I could do Thursday afternoon at 2PM. :) Does Hip Local Coffee Shop work for you?

Michael: Sounds great! I'll see you there! :)

• • •

WHO AM I? AND WHY AM I WRITING THIS BOOK?

Hey there, my name is Michael Boothby, and I used to be terrible at dating and terrified of communicating with other people. I'm guessing if you picked this book up that you are or used to be too.

Back in high school, I read books like *The Game* by Neal Strauss and found myself particularly drawn to pick-up artist culture which often uses social psychology to teach men how to manipulate women into sleeping with them.

Remember: I was young, shy, in high school and full of so many hormones I didn't know what to do with them all.

Reading these books cultivated an interest in psychology and brought me a heightened awareness of myself and how I was showing up to women, but the advice often felt impersonal and too *strategic*. There were a lot of strategies on how to get attention from women (and sleep with them), but not a lot about how to make actual connections and let your personality shine in an authentic way. In fact, many of these authors promoted a one-size-fits-all approach which, in my experience, doesn't work.

Just like how those infomercials told us that if we bought a Bowflex, we'd all turn into Greek Gods and Goddesses.

It was all a bunch of marketing bologna! And I hate bologna, and I don't want to feed you that crap!

The truth is we are all unique in how we learn, what we like and dislike, and how we choose to express our personalities through our communication. What works for one person may not work for another. The one constant that exists within all these variables is our choice to express ourselves, and we all possess the tools to express ourselves. Although these tools exist within us, we often discover them outside of ourselves. For example, I learned to express myself on the stage.

Since getting cast in the lead role in my sixth grade play (still the biggest role I've ever had), I've been in love with the stage and performing. I loved the attention I got being on stage and even more so, I loved how ALIVE I felt performing. I grew up playing video games and kept mostly to myself except for a few best friends (who also loved to play video games). Other people in school knew me, but I was never popular by traditional standards.

I had a few girlfriends in high school and college, but my relationships never lasted more than a few months. I always got bored or just didn't see the point of the relationship.

I also have to chime in at this point and say that I am unique in that I grew up with a twin sister who was and still is my best friend. We actually lived together in college, and I know this had an effect on my relationships and hers. I found that with all of my companionship needs being met, all I was really interested in was sex.

Perhaps this is why all those pickup artist books and products appealed to me. Sex was the one area of my life that I wanted to explore and felt that I didn't know how to. I'm sure many men have felt the same in their past.

I grew up with three sisters and always found myself drawn to women. Many of my close friends in high school and college were women. I always felt more comfortable around women than men. Perhaps this is because my father is a gynecologic oncologist, and he spent most of his time talking to women. Or maybe it's because I wasn't the most athletic guy and often felt intimidated around other men.

The point is: I was really great at befriending women, but I had a hard time *attracting* women and speaking my truth around women who I felt attracted towards. I was scared of rejection, and I was scared of losing the friendships I already had.

I didn't lose my virginity until I was 19. Even throughout college, I felt sexually inexperienced and always felt like I was missing out on some big secret that everyone else knew, and I didn't. Perhaps this was all just my own insecurity. We're all insecure about something.

I didn't know there was more to dating than sex, and it wasn't until I found myself in a loving relationship two years ago that I realized I wanted something more. I wanted a deeper connection, and I wanted to be better at communicating with my partner as well as with everyone in my life who I cared about. I had only had glimpses of genuine, deep connections with others, and it started back in college in an improvisational theater class.

I fell in love with improvisational theater because it allowed me to engage my imagination and creativity by playing with others, and I was able to create immediate connections with the people I performed with. I saw how in eight weeks, a room full of strangers became a room full of best friends with our own inside jokes to boot. I witnessed myself becoming more social and others as well, and I felt more in touch with myself and my self-expression. Communication didn't seem so scary anymore, and I began to take more risks in my life.

> **I got out of my head, trusted my gut, and followed my heart.**

I realized the same tools that helped me on stage could be applied to dating. When I discovered Tinder in college, I took my improviser's mind out to play and began to immediately see results. I'll come back to this in a bit because I want to tell you more about myself before we dive right in.

I recently moved through a severe depression and also had a spiritual awakening and realized we are all One. We are all searching for a sense of fulfillment in our lives, and we all desire a sense of belonging. We all also share the same struggles (we just don't like to talk about them as much).

If you believe we are all One, then every date you go on, you're really just meeting a different part of yourself. Don't like that person? It's probably because they are reflecting a part of yourself you don't like. That person was amazing? It's probably because they are reflecting that part of yourself that you also find amazing. We're all mirrors of each other.

Okay, that's all the woo-woo you're going to get in this book, and even if you don't believe we are all One, I'm sure you can agree that we can at least learn a lot from the people we interact with in our life? I know I've had moments when I've felt frustrated with society and dreamt of living off in a cave somewhere far away from other humans, but if I ever did, I'd just be with myself! I'd have no one to talk to or learn from or teach. I'd also probably die in a week because I grew up in Suburban Florida and have no wilderness survival skills whatsoever.

What I do have is awareness, and I want to bring more awareness to the field of dating and to the world. I think if we were all a little more aware of ourselves and others, the world would be a better place.

I also know it's easy to give advice; it's a lot harder to truly practice what you preach. Trust me, I am not perfect – just ask my girlfriend. She'll tell you about all the mistakes I've made in our relationship. I, however, choose to learn from my mistakes, improve, and become a better partner and hopefully a better human all around.

At the moment, I am writing this book and building a business, and I am scared.

I'm scared no one will read this book or people will read it and not like it. I'm scared people will think I'm a fraud. I'm scared I will fail. I'm scared all the time and energy I've invested into this book and my business will be for nothing. At the same time, though, I'm scared of succeeding and all the responsibility that comes with that.

Despite all this fear though, I keep waking up, (brushing my teeth), and working on this book. I've rewritten this introduction at least five times because everytime I read what I wrote, it didn't feel like me. It felt like me trying to be somebody else, and if that's how I started this book it would be a disservice both to you and myself because this book is all about teaching you how to best be you!

Yes, this book is about simplifying the Swipe Dating experience, but it is also about learning how to communicate authentically and express yourself effortlessly, so that you may connect with others more often (on the apps and in your life). It's also about how to use your creativity to create more fun and joyful interactions.

And who doesn't want more joy in their life?

I appreciate you taking the time to read this book and learn about me and more importantly to learn about yourself.

I chose to write this book about Online Dating because I find the topic infinitely interesting. It's been around now for around twenty years in various forms and iterations, but Online Dating is a rapidly changing landscape, and quite frankly...

It's *pretty weird*.

You have to write about yourself in a way that expresses your personality but also attracts the kind of person you actually want to hang out with. You have to post pictures that showcase your life and what you're all about. Then you have to look through a bunch of strangers' pictures and bios who also probably have no idea what they're doing. Next you have to craft that perfect message that expresses interest but isn't *too* forward, create something that resembles a conversation you'd have with someone in person, and then ask that person out on an ACTUAL DATE. Finally, meet up with that person and pretend like you both didn't just meet online.

It'll probably take tens or even hundreds of dates (not to mention messages) to find someone who is as weird as you are, truly loves themselves, and loves you for who you are.

And that's okay.

It's okay because **dating is a practice,** and as I've already stated, it is one of the best tools to learn about yourself and others.

You can learn what you like...and what you don't like. You can make a fool out of yourself (I know I have on many occasions). You can do whatever you want, really. It's all a process of trial and error and...

You're in it for the long haul.

You do your best to remain unattached to the end result because you know the outcomes don't matter in the long run. The process is everything.

My favorite comedian, Bill Hicks, once said,

"The world is like a ride in an amusement park. And when you choose to go on it, you think it's real because that's how powerful our minds are. And the ride goes up and down and round and round. It has thrills and chills and it's very brightly coloured and it's very loud and it's fun, for a while.

"Some people have been on the ride for a long time and they begin to question, is this real, or is this just a ride? And other people have remembered, and they come back to us, they say, 'Hey – don't worry, don't be afraid, ever, because, this is just a ride…"

We forget that sometimes, and dating online and off is one of the wildest rides there is.

Might as well enjoy it and learn a thing or two along the way.

I AGREE BUT AM IMPATIENT. WHAT EXACTLY WILL I LEARN IN THIS BOOK?

In this book, you will learn...

1. How to write and design an authentic and expressive profile

2. How to send an effective first message

3. How to have a memorable conversation through the app

4. How to smoothly transition to set up a date

5. How to have a successful first date

6. How to manage your expectations and stay motivated while single in the 21st Century

THAT ALL SOUNDS GREAT. CAN YOU HELP ME WITH THIS PROCESS YOURSELF?

Yes, I offer Complimentary Breakthrough Sessions.

You can get more information on the next page or just book a session right now.

Set up your complimentary session today[1]

---

1 https://calendly.com/michaelboothbycreative/15min

BREAKTHROUGH SESSION INVITATION

Are you ready to go on more dates?

Are you ready to express yourself more and learn about yourself in the process?

The only question I ask in my no-pitch session is "tell me about yourself."

This is not a sales call.

My only intention is to see if and how I can help you with your dating life.

Due to time constraints, the call must be limited to 15-minutes.

Are you ready to get started?

Set up your complimentary session today[2]

---

2 https://calendly.com/michaelboothbycreative/15min

HOW WILL I GET THE MOST OUT OF THIS BOOK?

By reading it, doing all the exercises, and practicing!

If you're new to Swipe Dating Apps, make a profile and try it all out!

If you've been in it for awhile and haven't been getting the results you wanted, try rewriting your profile or using the messaging tips to communicate in a new, more creative way! You'll never know until you try it out, and if what you're doing isn't working, you might as well try something new!

Think of this book like a little "quickstart guide" to Swipe Dating Apps or "Online Dating for Dummies" except I don't think you're a dummy!

When I started writing this book back in 2016, I was only using Tinder as it was the most popular Swipe Dating App at the time.

I do recognize that now, in 2019, there are even more options including Bumble, OKCupid, Plenty of Fish, Badoo, Tastebuds, and Hinge. There is even one called JSwipe which is for Jewish People or Non-Jewish people looking for a Jewish partner. I also found another one called Slide which is a Christian Swipe Dating App.

So there is truly an app out there for everyone now.

It is now possible to meet your future partner while lying in bed in your pajamas eating Ben and Jerry's.

Just how nature intended you to meet your mate.

Wait a minute.

None of this is natural at all!

It's *so weird*!

I know! And guess what? You're *weird* too! And so am I! And so are all the people you're going to meet. We're all *weird*!

HEY! I'M NOT THAT WEIRD, AND I STILL WANT TO KNOW MORE ABOUT YOU AND YOUR EXPERIENCE WITH SWIPE DATING APPS!

Alright "Normal Person" ;)

I'll happily satisfy your curiosity. Again, my name is Michael, and I'm a little over 28 years old as of writing this sentence. I am a writer, improviser, comedian, and musician who has been fascinated by Tinder since its release.

Back in 2013, I was in my third year of college at the University of Florida and, as you now know, not great at dating. I had plenty of friends at this point in my life and would go out to bars and parties every weekend but never had consistent success in my dating life. I was a voracious reader though and since the age of 15, I have read many self-help books like *The Power of Now*, *How to Win Friends and Influence People*, and *Escape from Cubicle Nation*.

Fun fact: I read *Escape from Cubicle Nation* before ever even having been in a cubicle.

As I mentioned earlier, in high school I read a lot of dating advice books; however, beyond not totally agreeing with their methods, I fell into the trap of feeling like I was learning by reading but not actually taking action and practicing the teachings (Looking back, it's a good thing I didn't practice some of those).

The first time I actually took action was when I listened to an episode of a dating show called "The Ask Women Podcast"[3] by Marni Kinrys, a dating coach whose books I have read and whose content I had found helpful and inspiring (I also recently appeared on Episode 276[4] talking about How to Succeed Online!). She recommended any guy who was single to jump on Tinder because it was an easy way to increase your odds of meeting women and going out on dates. That seemed like a low risk and high reward to me. I was already writing boring essays every week about U.S. Foreign Policy in the 20th Century and U.S.-Middle East Relations. Surely I could take my writing skills and apply some creativity to get a date or two.

Out at parties, I struggled with expressing myself openly and authentically and often felt nervous around attractive women. I frequently felt stuck in my head, which prevented me from being present and playful with women. Over the app though, I felt less pressure, and it was easy for me to express myself.

---

3 https://www.winggirlmethod.com/podcast/
4 https://poddtoppen.se/podcast/651219242/ask-women-podcast-what-women-want/ep-276-how-to-succeed-online-best-practice-tips-ad vice

Writing analytical essays every week about Containment Theory and the Cold War wasn't exactly sexy. I actually wrote a 45-page Honors Thesis about U.S.-French Relations in the Postwar Period after World War II and U.S. Ambassador to France, David Bruce, and his role in the Postwar Reconstruction.

Even now, as I sit here at my keyboard writing this, I can hear several of your heads hitting the desk at the mere description of my Thesis. I hear a symphony of collective snores as well.

My least favorite question back in college was "What are you writing your thesis about?"

I still hate when people ask me.

I didn't write for two years after finishing that damn Thesis. This book was actually the first writing project I got excited about again in my adult life.

It feels good to be excited about things.

And you know what else is exciting!? Going on first dates! And I went on so many more after discovering Tinder.

These dates provided opportunities to play with others, and as Plato once said, "You can learn more about a person in an hour of play than in a year of conversation."

I now know Plato's words to be true, because I've lived them out on every successful date I went on. I allowed myself to just "be myself" and play with the women I was with, and based on the outcomes, I believe play is the secret to attracting somebody *you actually want to be with.*

Tinder also allowed me the opportunity to play with my writer's brain and get creative with my first message to potential dates.

In the beginning, my process was one of trial and error. My best friend, Walter, and I would write raps and poems to girls to stand out. When we "got a match" we would sometimes even write an opening message for each other just for fun. We called this a "celeb shot" for those familiar with the classic college drinking game Beer Pong.

We didn't take the app seriously, and I don't think many of the women we talked to back then did either. However, now Tinder is serious business. In researching this book, I talked to hundreds of people who met their current partner on the app and others like it. I want to help you do the same!

I also want to make Swipe Dating Apps better and easier for everyone to use. I think the more people who can communicate and express themselves honestly and in a playful manner, the better the world will be. And people will end up going on more and better dates.

As a single guy in his twenties, I always loved going on first dates. It's exciting meeting someone you are interested in and learning about them and having them learn about you.

The butterflies in your stomach!

The anticipation!

The conversation!

Even if the date doesn't end up going the way you planned (which happens), there's always something new to discover and at the *very* least you leave with a fun story to share with your friends.

When I first began using Tinder back in 2013, nobody really understood how to use it or what it was. Although Swipe Dating Apps have been out now for nearly seven years, I feel that many still don't understand them or have preconceived notions of what they are for.

While Tinder was originally released for the college demographic as a hookup app, I believe it has evolved into much more than that. Through my experiences with the app, I have had one night stands, friends with benefits, and relationships.

I've even met some of my best friends through the app while travelling abroad.

Recently, I talked to a woman who got an engineering internship in Brussels through a conversation with a guy she met on Tinder, and they NEVER EVEN MET IN REAL LIFE.

In my opinion then…

> **Tinder is an efficient way to meet new people who you are attracted to and may or may not connect with.**
>
> **Nothing more, nothing less.**

You really can't know someone until you've spent time with them. You and I have just begun to spend some time together… Which leads me to…

WHY SHOULD YOU TRUST ME? WHAT MAKES ME QUALIFIED TO TEACH ANYONE?

Last time I checked, they're not exactly handing out PhDs in Tinderology at Harvard. If they were though, I would totally teach a class on it! I don't think I need to wear a suit and a tie and stand at the front of a lecture hall to teach anyone though.

In fact, I share the information in this book with anyone I meet who has questions about Swipe Dating Apps! I've been using Tinder since it came out, and although I am now in a committed relationship, I learned a lot when I was single.

Full disclosure: I am not a guru. I'm just a regular guy who created a more successful dating life for himself and met many amazing women through Swipe Dating Apps. I am a performer and do believe I may be more charismatic than the average person, but I also believe anyone can do anything they put their mind to. I also believe everyone has the ability to create and express themselves.

I learned how to best communicate over the digital medium through an exploratory process of trial and error. I've taken everything I've learned from my experiences with the app and coupled it with my knowledge of improvisational theater, stand-up comedy, and working in sales to create this book.

This book started as an experiment of sorts while I was living abroad in New Zealand. I had just moved to Wellington and wanted to go on more dates to explore the local bars and restaurants. In a good week, I could set up three or four dates. I found that scheduling too many dates in a week stressed me out though, so I began to scale back.

My roommates at the time were big gamers and didn't get out much (they reminded me of a former version of myself), and I often "Tinder'd" in the living room. They saw me using the app frequently and going on so many dates, and they asked how I was having so much success.

In a fit of passion I replied, "Guys, it's simple!"

I grabbed a pen and a piece of paper and started writing everything:

1.   Write an Expressive Profile.
2.   Swipe Until You Get A Match.
3.   Send a Unique First Message
4.   Create a Fun Conversation.
5.   Ask for the Date. Be Specific.
6.   Show Up and Be Present.

I looked down at what I wrote, and like Einstein discovering the Theory of Relativity, I screamed out, "Eureka!"

Okay, I didn't do that, but I said, "This has to be a book! This information could help a lot of people!"

So I woke up every morning at 7AM for a month and wrote like a man possessed. I guided my roommates along the way.

I helped them design their profiles. Soon they started getting matches. Then I helped them write their first messages. Then I helped them carry on a conversation. Then I gave them tips for their first date and sent them on their way!

They soon started having consistent success as well. They not only began going on more dates, but they also became more social and satisfied with their lives. When I saw this transformation, I knew I was onto something.

If you're already having success with the Swipe Dating Apps or dating in general, then great, keep doing what you're doing! You probably don't need advice from me or anyone else. Although more knowledge and feedback never hurt anyone ;)

The information in this book helped my old roommates, and I know it can help you too if you're open to receiving it and willing to commit to the exercises and to do the work.

> **If you are open to it, this book has the power to not only improve your dating life, but your relationship with yourself and with every single person in your life.**

Hopefully we'll share a few laughs along the way as well. I find humor in everything, and I encourage you to as well :)

OKAY, I'M IN, BUT WHY SWIPE DATING APPS?

Simply put, Swipe Dating Apps are the easiest way to get a date if you live in a city. Honestly, if you live in a rural area, this book may not help you out that much. I've used Tinder in rural areas before, and the sample size is so small, you will probably match with people you already know. If you haven't used them before though, feel free to go for it.

If you really want to experience the abundance of Swipe Dating Apps, I would suggest moving to a city if possible. If you can't move to a city, you can still try out the apps, but you'll probably have to date the old fashioned way and find dates by meeting people through friends or work or any other activity in your town where people get together.

With Swipe Dating Apps, you just log into your smartphone and start swiping. You can set the search radius, so you only see people near you or you can include people further away. If you've been out of your house in the last few years, you will have noticed that almost everybody is on their smartphone: walking down the street, waiting in line at the grocery store, hiking in the woods, even sitting in the movie theater when you're trying to enjoy the movie (Those jerks!).

Everywhere you go you will find people tapping away, so you may as well go where the people are like the Little Mermaid wanted to[5]. As I said earlier, I know there are many other Swipe Dating Apps out on the market now, but Tinder is still one of the most popular with an estimated user base of 57 million people, 1.6 billion swipes per day which result in 1 million dates per week. Those numbers are nothing to shake a stick at, and if you're single and not going on any dates, you have no excuses to not be on these apps.

---

5 https://www.youtube.com/watch?v=0UBqDqKWKJo

WHO AM I WRITING THIS BOOK FOR?

In general, I'm writing this book for anyone who is confused about Swipe Dating Apps and wants to go on more dates.

I had several specific audiences in mind as well.

I'm writing first and foremost for all the young guys out there who are confused about communication: the guys who find themselves at a loss for what to say and want to avoid cheap jokes or sounding creepy. I genuinely believe most of these guys are good guys; however, through the anonymity given by the app they falsely believe they can skip regular social conventions and be direct to the point that it comes across as straight creepy. If you are a guy who sends creepy messages, please read this book first before you send another. It's not a long read, and you will actually go on more dates.

Secondly, I'm writing this book for older single guys who may be unfamiliar with how to use the Internet and dating apps and would like to improve their dating lives armed with the knowledge and best practices of this new technology.

Finally, I'm also writing this book for women. While I am a man and realize much of the advice in the book may benefit men more due to my male perspective, I've found through my research that many women enjoy initiating the first conversation. With apps like Bumble which empower women to send the first message, I believe all of the material in this book is applicable.

The material is all about creating a fun conversation from scratch that leads to a tangible date, and so, at its heart, this book is about open and authentic communication which I believe is Universal.

WHAT MAKES THIS BOOK DIFFERENT FROM OTHER BOOKS ABOUT TINDER AND ONLINE DATING?

I attempted to write this book for men **AND** women.

I've read several books on online dating and have found that they contain more bad and even disturbing advice than helpful and heart-centered advice. One book I read even suggested buying an SUV only to have sex in the back of it with a women right away after the date. Why? This is a problem.

And so, this book aims to be more about conversation than procreation.

> **Although if procreation occurs because of quality conversation and mutual attraction and consent, all the better!**

Secondly, this book is **not** only anecdotal. I will be sharing stories from my dating life, but I also have data to support my conclusions. In my research for this book, I conducted an anonymous online survey that analyzed various aspects of a standard Tinder interaction and collected results from men and women around the world. I've also learned a great deal from performing standup comedy, performing and teaching improvisational theater, and working in sales. Performing and selling require confidence, open-mindedness, adaptability, creativity, active-listening skills, and practice. Dating will challenge you in all of these areas as well, and there will be opportunities to learn and practice throughout the book.

Excerpts from the anonymous surveys are used directly in Chapter 3, so feel free to skip ahead if your curiosity has the better of you. You can always come back to Chapter 1. Honestly you can jump to any part of the book if you want. If you think you already have a great profile designed and are fine at messaging but need some work on setting up dates, start at Chapter 4. Use this book however you want to get the most value out of it.

You can also find a selection of the anonymous survey results in Appendix 2.

WHAT WILL THIS BOOK COVER MORE SPECIFICALLY?

I know I already laid out the outline of what you'll be learning in this book, but I want to also address common fears and skepticism about Online Dating and Swipe Dating Apps first. While Online Dating has been around now for almost two decades, many who have not used it before may feel nervous or apprehensive. This is natural. I believe when it comes to Online Dating, you should always trust your gut. **ALWAYS** meet your date in public first, and if you have a bad feeling about someone, trust your instincts and leave at any time.

Another common concern that people have is that someone they meet will be boring or that they themselves are boring. You can't say for certain if someone is worth your time until you've met up with them in person. If you're denouncing everyone you see on the app as boring then you'll never really know. Try to go into dates with an open mind.

If you feel that *you* are boring, take the time to discover what you like and develop hobbies and interests around that. After all, if you don't like yourself, why should anyone else? And if you don't LOVE yourself, why should anyone else?

Tough love, but it's true.

I would also tell you that *everyone* is pretty boring. Look at any great stand-up comedian. Are they talking about how they climbed Mount Everest and went to space? No. They're talking about their boring lives or their observations of other people's boring lives. They just find the funny in it all, and you are 100% capable of doing the same!

The main goal of this book though is to teach you how to **message with purpose** on Swipe Dating Apps and in "real life."

What do I mean by that?

I mean you must always know what and why you are sending a message before you send it. You want to meet up with someone you are interested in? Great! Well to do that you must first ask yourself what you want to get out of Swipe Dating Apps. A one night stand? A friend? A friend with benefits? A relationship? A future husband/wife? A late night milkshake drinking partner?

WHATEVER IT IS YOU'RE LOOKING FOR, YOU CAN FIND IT ON SWIPE DATING APPS, BUT TO FIND IT, YOU MUST MESSAGE WITH PURPOSE.

The second goal is to teach you how to sell yourself. As much as I hate to admit it, dating and much of life is all about being able to sell your ideas and your personality. You could be the most amazing person, but if you don't know how to present yourself to other people and express your personality, you won't get far in life. This book will teach you how to express yourself with ease by being both interesting and interested.

> **Pro tip:**
> **being interested in others will make you interesting ;)**

In the case of Swipe Dating Apps, you will learn how to design a profile that people will want to swipe right for. You will also learn how to send messages that get responses. I don't want to turn you into a robotic dating salesman though. I want you to be able to express yourself genuinely. This is where my improvisation and performance background comes in. The better you can express yourself through written (and oral) communication and be present, the better equipped you will be to find someone who likes you for you. This is true on and off Swipe Dating Apps.

The final goal is to teach you how to stay motivated and manage your expectations when you're single. Not all dates will go as planned, and you want to be able to bounce back from the bad ones. Some dates will go really well, and you may feel a lot of intense positive emotions. You want to be able to maintain a healthy neutrality about it all and act appropriately in both scenarios and every scenario in between, so you don't hurt yourself or somebody else emotionally.

At the end of the day when you're single, *it's all about you.*

Finally I want to make a disclaimer:

If you are depressed or going through a rough time, I wouldn't recommend using Swipe Dating Apps.

Going on dates can be an easy cover up for your pain and a nice distraction, but you'll only be projecting your sadness and problems onto other people which isn't fair to them. Seek the help that you need first. I'm speaking from experience here. I spent three years in therapy, have attended several Ayahuasca Ceremonies, and now practice a regular meditation and breathwork routine. I've found what works for me to be comfortable with myself.

Whatever you have to do to be okay, do it. Whoever you have to talk to, talk to them. Your life is all you have, and without that, without the joy and support that comes from a community, from being healthy, it's hard to even think about dating or supporting someone else.

WHAT WILL THIS BOOK NOT COVER?

This book will not give you pickup lines or any canned material. I cannot tell you what to write or say specifically because I am not you. I will show examples of successful conversations that I have had that led to dates, but I urge you to use these only as inspiration. Everybody has a different personality and conversational style. **I want to help you discover yours**.

Again, this book is **not** a guide to getting laid. There are no simple tips or tricks. More importantly, *no one is a prize to be won*. We are all human beings, and it just so happens that when human beings connect with each other sometimes they also like to have sex. If you have more sex after reading this book, it's only because you've become a more honest and expressive person and are connecting with more people you are interested in.

HOW DO I DEFINE A CONNECTION? A METAPHOR FOR ONLINE DATING

A connection is any link between two people. If I threw a ball at you, and you caught it, and threw it back, we've just connected even if only on a shallow level. You've looked at me, acknowledged the game, and decided you want to play.

If I threw a ball at you, and you caught it but didn't throw it back, you've said you may want to connect. You've acknowledged me, but you're not sure if you want to play with me yet. You might throw the ball back or hold onto it forever or throw it into the street in front of an oncoming car (which would be kinda rude).

If I threw a ball at you, and it hit you, you probably should've been paying more attention to your surroundings which brings us back the REAL point of this book: to increase your *awareness*.

By the end, my hope is you will know how to throw the ball, catch it, and throw it back when it's been thrown at you (if that's what you want).

The whole ball throwing metaphor is also a great example of consent which is ESSENTIAL in all forms of dating.

WHEN DO HUMAN BEINGS CONNECT?

All the time. Every day you have the potential to connect with somebody else through your actions and reactions to the environment and the people in it. All it takes is a willingness to put yourself out there. You never know what or who might come back your way!

CAN WE GET ON WITH THE BOOK ALREADY???

As Obama said back in '08, "Yes, we can!"

Let's begin with the first message you will send to the world on Swipe Dating apps: your profile.

This Page Unintentionally Left Blank

(See What Happens When You Message without Purpose?)

CHAPTER 1

STAND OUT FROM THE PACK. EXPRESS YO'SELF!

EVERYDAY EXPRESSION AND YOU

Every day, you wake up, brush your teeth (if you care about your dental health), take a shower, pick out what clothes you want to wear, and style your hair in some fashion. Maybe you take one look at your hair in the mirror and decide to wear a hat instead. Maybe you slept through your alarm, and now you only have time to hastily throw on some clothes and rush out the door. If you're a woman, maybe there's even more to your routine. As a brother to three sisters, I often observed them taking more time than I did to get ready putting on makeup, blow drying their hair and styling it, and overall just caring more about their outfit than I did. As a woman, you might spend more time in your routine doing these extra steps, or you might be like me and really not care and just be going for comfort.

The point is: before you even step out of the house in the morning, whether you are a man or a woman, you probably put some time into your appearance. The way you present yourself to the world, your self expression, whether you are conscious of it or not, affects the way the world reacts to you. Before you even open your mouth to talk to anyone, people will look at you and make a judgment. People will initiate conversations with you or respond to your initiations largely based on how you look.

Imagine you're at a bus stop, and a man comes up to you and asks if he can borrow some change. If this man smells, has a scraggly beard, and is wearing dirty clothes, you'd probably assume he was homeless and just begging for money. You'd probably feel uncomfortable and tell him you don't have any change or ignore him all together; maybe you have a kind heart and toss him a dollar or two. Maybe he keeps bothering you, and you decide to keep walking and catch the bus at the next stop.

Now imagine another man comes up to you and asks if he can borrow some change. This man smells like an angel, is well groomed and wearing a sharp, blue suit. You'd probably assume he lost his wallet (maybe he explained that he did) and help him with his fare home. Maybe you were listening to music while swiping through Tinder and you didn't even hear him ask, leaving him to awkwardly pretend like he said nothing at all. That's never happened to me before…

Here's a real and more personal example of physical appearance affecting communication. Back in 2016 when I lived in Wellington, New Zealand, my day job was doing face-to-face fundraising on the streets for charity.

Yes, I was one of *those* people: a charity mugger.

Strangers saw me from a block away with my bright shirt and iPad ready to strike up a conversation and sign them up for monthly donations. Naturally, when I said, "Hi!" I got a range of responses. Sometimes they would say nothing and keep walking, knowing that if they engaged with me, I would pitch them. Sometimes they would smile and say hi back… and then keep walking because they wanted to appear polite but also didn't want to be pitched. Sometimes they would look me in the eye, shake their head because they knew I wanted their money, and keep walking. Every now and then, someone would actually stop and talk to me.

Now imagine if instead of selling charity to people, I was selling $1 donuts, and I had three cute puppies with me. Everybody would be stopping to chat! Because who doesn't love cheap donuts and puppies!?

People who are crazy fitness nuts and hate cuteness!

But nobody wants to hang out with those people anyways!

FIRST IMPRESSIONS ARE EVERYTHING: WHAT MESSAGES ARE YOU SENDING ACROSS TO POTENTIAL DATES?

Obviously every time you log in to a Swipe Dating App, you don't have to dress yourself or mentally prepare for a day of rejection selling charity (lucky for you!). Hell, you can go for a swipe buck naked in your bedroom for all I care! What you do have to prepare for though is what messages your profile is sending across to potential matches.

Before you even start swiping and sending messages on Swipe Dating Apps, you should invest some time into making a profile that stands out. Your profile is the **FIRST IMPRESSION** people have of you, and you want to make sure you're expressing yourself in a way that is genuine, attractive, and inviting.

Think of your profile as an advertisement for yourself. You are the product that wants to be bought (matched with).

Who is your target market (ideal date)?

Does your profile represent yourself accurately?

Does this representation of yourself appeal to the type of person who you'd like to actually spend time with?

A well-made profile will increase your matches and therefore your opportunities to go on more dates and connect with people you are interested in (and who are hopefully interested in you). Ideally, a well-made profile should do **TWO** things:

1. Give potential dates an idea of who you are and what you're about while not giving away the whole story.

2. Provide "conversational breadcrumbs" that give potential dates an easy way to start a conversation with you.

It's important that your profile checks both boxes. You want to put your personality in the spotlight while also not making it difficult for potential dates to reach out to you. I call this "Breadcrumb Theory."

Like Hansel and Gretel, you want to leave a trail of breadcrumbs for interested people to follow but don't reveal the final destination right off the bat. Hopefully this trail leads to you two connecting on an amazing date and not being cooked alive and eaten by a cannibalistic witch.

Perhaps a better analogy would be "Create Your Tinder Profile like an Adult Coloring Book." Give potential matches an outline of who you are but keep them guessing. Then when you're both finally out on a date you can color your books in together :)

> **ACTION:** The best thing you can do right now to see if your profile is up to par is to ask yourself: "What does my profile say about me?" Look at your profile as if you were a random person looking at it. Can you notice your personality from your pictures and bio? If after looking at your own profile, you can't easily answer these questions, it's time to do a little work.

THE "LOST ART" OF SELF EXPRESSION OR LAZINESS?

Through my years of swiping I've read more Tinder profiles than I can count. While a few stood out to me, many blended in with the rest. How could this be? Are most Tinder Users just boring people living boring lives? Maybe, but I refuse to believe that.

I believe that most just don't know how to best express themselves with only six pictures and a bio or are too lazy to take the time. I'm sure many download Tinder, use the pictures that are automatically taken from their Facebook and dive right in. I understand that some may not want to invest a lot of time into their profile, but if you want to increase your chances of meeting up and connecting with people, you should at least put a little effort into it.

I've seen many profiles that use all six pictures but have no bio, and their pictures don't really tell me much about who they are. Or their pictures send a message that's unattractive and uninteresting. Really? Six selfies in a row? Either your only friend is your smartphone or you are a direct descendant of Narcissus[6]…neither sounds like they would be much fun on a date!

I've also seen Tinder profiles where the User wrote a bio but used a throwaway line like "I don't know what I'm doing here" or "My friends made me make an account" or "I made this when I was drunk." Again, these lines express **NOTHING** about your personality and in fact indicate confusion, doubt, and regret right off the bat. Using a line like this in your bio is like walking into a party and shouting out, "I don't actually want to be here! My friends dragged me here! This party sucks!" And, again, who wants to hang out with that person? I know I don't, and I hope you don't either.

---

6 https://www.ancient.eu/Narcissus/

Another line that I see often is some variation of "I don't know how to describe myself." Again, saying this in your bio does you no favors unless you are actively looking for a writing coach or advice on how to express yourself. I'm sure you've seen countless profiles with no bios or bios that fail to entertain, inform, or enlighten potential dates in any way, shape, or form. Let's do better!

HOW DO I BEST EXPRESS MYSELF THROUGH A SWIPE DATING APP BIO?

I assume most people know how to write a resume or a cover letter for a job and can talk about themselves enough in interviews to be employed (most of the women I went out with on Tinder had jobs). Usually this kind of writing is sterile. You want to list your achievements without bragging too much while also listing your skills and qualifications. Employers want to be able to look at this piece of paper and know immediately if you "make the grade." Don't write your Tinder bio like a resume. Instead, try to write your bio like that of a comedian.

I am a comedian. As a comedian, I should write a bio to send to producers if I ever want to get booked for gigs. A good comedy bio describes your style of humor and the content of your act. Additionally, you must infuse your personality into your writing. Ideally it should be written in the same voice you perform with. Approach your Swipe Dating App Bio with this same mindset.

I know most people are not comedians, but most people do want to go on dates with other people they find interesting.

You may not have an act and a stage persona, but you do have a personality and a unique voice. If you don't know what it is, try asking yourself these questions:

If you asked your best friend to describe you in three words, what would they say?

What phrases or expressions do you love to use and why?

What are you passionate about?

I DON'T GET THE IDEA, PLEASE ELABORATE!

Your Tinder Bio does not have to be your life story. In fact, I would advocate you don't write your life story. No one has the time or energy to read that, and you want to leave plenty to talk about on the first date. You do want to stand out from other people though and give potential dates a taste of what you are like in person.

Referencing pop culture gives people an easy way to start a conversation with you, especially if you're both fans of the same thing. If you can incorporate pop culture into your own joke or catchphrase or saying, even better.

If you like Harry Potter, you could say something like "It's not the wand, it's the wizard!" or "I'm a Slytherin who wishes he was Gryffindor..."

Or if you're a Star Wars fan you could start your profile by saying, "A long time ago, in a galaxy far, far away..."

Or if you're a fan of The Shining, you could say, "HEEEEERE'S JOHNNNNNY!"

On second thought, maybe skip that last one, but you get the idea.

ACTION: Write or rewrite your Tinder Bio infused with your personality. Keep it concise; don't ramble or waste words. Remember: Canned lines and jokes are okay but not great. If you are using a line that others are using, you're missing the first opportunity to express yourself in a unique way to potential dates.

THE PICTURE-PERFECT FORMULA

What is the perfect picture formula?

There isn't one.

From all the profiles I've looked at over the years, it seems that most people include the same types of photos:

"Oh look, here's a photo of me travelling."

"Oh look, now I'm skydiving." (this might have just been a New Zealand thing)

"Oh look, here's me in a kayak in the distance where you can't even see what I look like."

This is fine if it's an accurate representation of who you are, but I'm going to guess it's not since I've seen so many other profiles with the same types of photos. I'm sure if you've been on these apps, you've also seen patterns in the types of photos that men and women post. This book is all about better expressing yourself over the digital medium. I can't tell you which photos best represent you, but I can give you a template to follow if you don't know where to begin:

1. A nice picture of your face with a natural smile in good light. This is your most important photo as it's the first people will see while swiping. This is your Calling Card. I don't think you need to use a professional headshot as that may be a bit too stuffy or pretentious. Your expression also may seem forced in a professional headshot. Keep it casual and simple. Additionally, avoid group photos for this one and leave the sunglasses and Halloween masks at home. Just you in all your glory!

2. A picture of you doing an activity you love by yourself. What are you passionate about? What are your hobbies? Again, the more expressive you are in your photos the better.

3. A picture of you doing another activity you love with friends. I think it's better to have a candid group photo than a staged one (i.e. prom photos, "going out" photos, etc). This photo is super important if you are a man. The group shot shows potential dates that you have friends and basic social skills and are not a serial killer. Or if you are, you're like Dexter and are good

at hiding it. Even Dexter had a wife and a kid. If he can, so can you.

4.   Another expressive photo of you doing another activity either alone or with friends.

5.   Wild Card 1: If you have pictures with cute animals, throw them in. Everyone loves cute animals, and it's an easy conversation starter.

6.   Wild Card 2: A photo of yourself expressing an emotion not seen in previous photos. What excites you? Makes you happy? Confuses you? Surprises you? Makes you upset? Your goal is to make it as easy as possible for interested people to start a conversation with you.

Again: this is just a basic template to follow if you have no idea where to start. You want to give potential dates an idea of who you are. Remember to be genuine. I wouldn't advocate taking photos of yourself doing cool things for the sake of looking "cool." If you just happen to be into "cool" things, by all means highlight them. If you don't think you can talk about the activity you're highlighting on a date at length though, I wouldn't post it. I doubt most people are adrenaline junky, skydiving, motorcycle riding rock stars/brain surgeons. If this person exists, they're either dead by now or too preoccupied with their glamorous, adventurous lifestyle to be swiping on Swipe Dating Apps.

PICTURES AS SHORT STORIES

Your photos should provide a glimpse into your life. A rule that is common amongst writers is "Show me, don't tell me." This is a good rule to follow for designing your profile as well. If you play guitar, don't say you love music and playing guitar, post a photo of yourself playing guitar and loving every second of it.

Do you love solving crossword puzzles? Take a photo of yourself solving crossword puzzles with a look of intense concentration. Love video games? Have a friend take a photo of yourself mid-game as you're passionately barking orders into your headset guiding your team to victory. Maybe you love knitting? In which case, take an action photo of yourself knitting or showing off a sweet scarf you made. The goal here is to capture the emotion in your face while doing an activity you are passionate about. You want people to react to your pictures. Be expressive, make strangers *feel* the emotions you felt at that moment in time.

> **ACTION:** Use photos that tell short stories about your life. Photos that grab attention, invite curiosity or comments. Photos of you being you. If you look at a photo of yourself and can't make an interesting observation or caption for it, don't use it.

DO I REALLY NEED A BIO?

No, you don't. You probably don't need a car to get to work, but it sure helps you get there faster. If you think your pictures alone give potential dates enough to talk about then by all means don't write a bio, but having a good bio will help.

Most of the women I talked to and surveyed told me they always read a man's bio before choosing to swipe right or left. Most of the men I talked to said they only really swipe through the photos at first before matching with a woman. When I was single, I would only read a woman's bio after matching with them. I did this to save time mostly but also to manage my expectations. I didn't want to read about how amazing or interesting someone was before we even matched. I did find it hard to write a good message though if I matched with someone, and their pictures were not expressive enough or they had no bio.

PUTTING IT ALL TOGETHER

After designing your profile infused with your personality, you should read it and immediately think, "Hell yeah! I would hang out with me! I'm interesting and awesome in my own unique way, and I'm going to find someone as equally interesting and awesome as me!"

Again, if you feel like you aren't interesting, discover what you love about life and yourself, and if you can, have a friend take photos of you doing the things you love! Or take fun, expressive selfies. Just know you don't have to travel the world to figure out what you love (although if you have the option to, go for it).

Give a new activity you've always wanted to try a shot.

Take a Salsa Class!

Teach yourself how to cook!

Take an Improv Class!

Improvisational Theater has been integral to my journey of self-development. So much so, that I now teach a class[7] here in Chicago where I combine improvisation with meditation and mindfulness practices. I also have incorporated improvisation into my dating coaching practices because every date you go on and every interaction you have is a co-created improvisation.

At the minimum, do something different every day to mix up your schedule. Go for a walk in the morning or in the evening, start a new workout regime, start practicing meditation and mindfulness, start journaling, do The Artist's Way[8].

Do anything! And I promise when you get back into the online dating game, you'll have a better idea of who you are and will be better equipped to write a more expressive profile.

---

7 https://www.meetup.com/chicagomindfulimprov/
8 https://www.amazon.com/Artists-Way-25th-Anniversary/dp/0143129252

ACTION: This might sound cheesy, but if you're having trouble writing about yourself, I want you to write a love letter to yourself. If you were another person who loved you, what would you write? What do *you* love about yourself and your life? Be honest and get creative! Remember, if you don't love yourself, why should anyone else?

Who knows? Maybe on your quest of self-discovery, you'll meet someone special and won't even need to re-download any dating apps! I talked to a new friend recently who said she met her husband right after uninstalling Tinder, so you never know!

But assuming you…

A) Haven't met someone special yet through a radical (or simple) quest of self-discovery

B) Have some idea of who you are, and…

C) Would like to increase your opportunities to meet and connect with interesting people

It's time to start swiping and matching!

And if you'd like some extra help on your journey, consider scheduling a Complimentary 15-minute Breakthrough Session with me[9].

CHAPTER SUMMARY

1. A well-made profile should...

    a. Give potential dates an *idea* of who you are and what you're about while not giving away the whole story.

    b. Provide **"conversational breadcrumbs"** that give potential dates an easy way to start a conversation with you

2. Infuse your personality into your bio. **Be original**. Use humor and reference pop culture (with a unique spin) if you can.

3. Infuse your personality into your pictures as well. The more expressive, the better. Each of your photos should tell a short story about your life.

---

9 https://calendly.com/michaelboothbycreative/15min

CHAPTER 2

"YOU'VE GOT A MATCH!" NOW WHAT?

1. Identify → *2. Shine* → *3. Play* → *4. Make Plans*

SWIPING STRATEGIES

Before we talk about sending the first message, let's talk about swiping. When it comes to swiping, there are many ways to do it. I use my thumb because it's practical, but I have a friend who uses his pinky, a more extravagant and slightly unnecessary move. Honestly, swipe with whatever finger feels best…or use your big toe if you are really feeling adventurous! When it comes to choosing to swipe left or right though, I would say you should also do what feels best. I can't tell you who or what you are attracted to. I can tell you how I personally approached swiping to save time though.

Unless I had a lot of time on my hands, I didn't usually read bios right off the bat. I would look at their profile picture and immediately decide if I was physically attracted to this person or not. Again, I did this to save time but also to manage my expectations. I didn't want to read about how amazing or interesting someone was and get my hopes up only to never match. Some might argue swiping only based on someone's profile picture is shallow; however, physical attraction is the only metric we really have to go on at this point in the process.

If you were out in public and saw someone you were attracted to, you would be making that decision based off of their looks and their style. Last time I checked people don't have tiny bios floating above their heads. Who knows though, maybe in ten years all our smartphones will be integrated into our eyes, and we'll actually swipe right on an app that's interfaced into the real world.

This is starting to sound like an episode of Black Mirror.

It seems like this is the direction we are headed technologically, but we're not there yet. We're in 2019, and Swipe Dating Apps only exist in our handheld smartphones.

Right now, swiping on an app is a much safer and risk-averse way to start a conversation with somebody you're attracted to. I know this is why I started using the apps and why they have gained so much popularity.

After I matched with someone, I would then take the time to read their bio to find inspiration for writing my first message.

SWIPING, MESSAGING STATISTICS AND YOU

Tinder statistics show that women swipe right 14% of the time whereas men swipe right 46% of the time. This statistic shows us that women are more selective in their swiping habits than men, and many of the women I surveyed said they always read the bio before swiping. As highlighted by my own personal swiping strategy above, men instinctively are more attracted to physical appearance alone, so this discrepancy in swiping statistics makes sense.

OKCupid founder, Christian Rudder, illustrates in his book Dataclysm that women receive exponentially more messages from men than men do from women. In the top 10% of "Attractiveness percentile" (a real metric) women received on average just under 5 messages a day whereas the most attractive men received less than one. If we extrapolate these numbers over to Tinder, we can estimate that women receive around five times as many messages as men. To even send a message on Tinder, you first must match, so it's safe to assume that women get around five times as many matches as men. If you're a man, these figures should show you why it is so important for your first message to stand out (in a positive way).

WHEN TO STOP SWIPING AND MESSAGE

All statistics notwithstanding, if you follow the tips outlined in the previous chapter about making a more expressive profile, you should be getting more matches than you were before, regardless of your gender.

Personally, I used to stop swiping to send messages after I got **three or four** matches. Feeling the endorphin rush when the screen pops up saying "You've Got a Match!" is exciting, and you may be tempted to keep swiping and accumulating matches and tiny ego boosts with reckless abandon.

I would discourage this though for several reasons.

First of all, I don't know about you, but multitasking stresses me out and trying to have three or four conversations at the same time is difficult enough. Also, if you have three or four matches, you can assume that not everyone will respond to you. If after sending three or four messages, you still don't get a response, don't dwell on it or beat yourself up, just keep on swiping. There are a million reasons why someone may not respond to your message, and there are plenty of fish in the sea!

Plenty of fish… That's a great name for a dating app! Oh wait...[10]

If you're still struggling with that first message, don't fret! We'll talk about how to improve your messaging in the next section.

I liked to send messages as soon as I matched though as not to get lost in the other person's pile. Sending a message right after matching is the best way *to stay relevant* and stand out. Remember, people are busy, and these Swipe Dating Apps are designed like games where every person is reduced to a card. Don't let yourself become another card. Stand out!

If you match with someone and don't message them straight away, what are you waiting for?

---

10 https://www.pof.com/

TO INITIATE THE CONVERSATION OR NOT?

If your match has not messaged you first, then it's safe to assume they are waiting for you to message them. If you are both waiting for the other person to message first, then there will never be a conversation at all, and you will miss your opportunity to potentially meet up and connect with someone you are interested in.

While the results of my anonymous survey showed that many women do now initiate the conversation, it seems many still prefer for men to make the first move. That being said, I think if you're interested in someone, by all means send them a message regardless of your gender. When I was single, I loved when a woman took the initiative and messaged me first, and I'm sure I'm not alone.

And not just a "Hey there :)" but a thoughtfully crafted first message.

I am aware that gender norms still exist though, and even in the world of online dating, they do still tend to shape behavior.

THE CASE OF CREEPY MATT OR WHAT NOT TO DO WHEN YOU HAVE A MATCH AND HAVE A PENIS

Meet "Creepy Matt." Creepy Matt messaged a friend of mine who took my anonymous survey who we will call Jill. Jill was gracious enough to send screenshots of the conversation to me.

Let's observe, shall we:

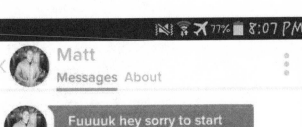

Matt

Messages About

Fuuuuk hey sorry to start this way but youre incredibly fucking hot

1 hour ago

You're allowed to start that way if you can bring it back to being normal

16 mins ago

Whats normal

15 mins ago

Haha fair. I guess I just mean be willing to meet up and have a chat

15 mins ago

What u looking for on here

14 mins ago

I don't promise or aim for

GIF Send a message...

I don't promise or aim for anything. Just meet up and see what happens

11 mins ago

Well im looking for you to be my friend that gives me some benefit could that

9 mins ago

You can't just go straight to sex dude. If we don't get along I'm not going to fuck you

9 mins ago

I get that

8 mins ago

So we could meet up and see where this goes if you want

4 mins ago

GIF | Send a message...

Matt

Messages About

4 mins ago

Tell me How do u like to be fucked

And i just have to say you do have a beautiful pair of x

3 mins ago

You don't seem to be understanding me

1 min ago

I do just tryna get to know u better

1 min ago

Getting to know me better is one thing. You're trying to get to fuck me quicker.

Ask a normal question

Now

GIF Send a message...

Matt
Messages About

8 hours ago

You don't seem to be understanding me

8 hours ago

I do just tryna get to know u better

8 hours ago

Getting to know me better is one thing. You're trying to get to fuck me quicker.

Ask a normal question

8 hours ago

What size is your bra and do u wear victoria secret?! They look amazing ;))

Come on

8 hours ago

GIF Send a message...

Clearly, "Creepy Matt" doesn't understand the fundamentals of communication over Tinder and quite possibly in real life. Observe how at every stage of the conversation, Jill even *gives* Matt an *easy* way to not be creepy and have a normal conversation that leads to a date. Which she didn't even have to do. And yet he carries on like a misogynistic, over eager cartoon character[11] from the 1940s.

This is Creepy Matt.

Guys: don't be like Creepy Matt. To not be like Creepy Matt, follow this one easy rule.

MY NUMBER ONE SWIPE DATING APP MESSAGING RULE THAT EVERYONE (BUT ESPECIALLY GUYS) SHOULD FOLLOW

This rule is mostly for the Creepy Matts out there. I find it hard to believe there are many Sarahs or Katies sending creepy messages on Swipe Dating Apps. And if there are Michaels out there sending creepy messages, stop it guys! You're ruining our reputation!

Here it is:

> If you wouldn't say it to someone in real life, don't say it online."

Say it again out loud with me:

> **"IF YOU WOULDN'T SAY IT TO SOMEONE IN REAL LIFE, DON'T SAY IT ONLINE."**

Did you say it loud enough? I CAN'T HEAR YOU!

Now I feel like the Captain in the introduction to Spongebob Squarepants. I wonder what kind of first messages that guy would send on Swipe Dating Apps?

Who cares!

Listen: People don't usually respond well to strangers saying creepy things about them. If you say creepy things on Swipe Dating Apps, you should listen to Dora the Explorer when she says,

"Swiper, no swiping!"

I know Dora was talking about a fox that steals things, but what are guys like Creepy Matt doing but stealing and wasting precious time while also making themselves look like incompetent and simple-minded human beings? If someone sends you a creepy message, send them the photo of the Misogynistic Wolf. Or send them a link to this book. Or any book for that matter.

Also, if anyone from Nickelodeon is reading this, please don't sue me.

TO START A GOOD CONVERSATION, INITIATE LIKE AN IMPROVISER

Now that we've had that conversation, let's talk about how to actually start a good conversation on Swipe Dating Apps.

I approached every online conversation like I was starting an improvisational theater scene.

In improv, your goal is to create a scene out of nothing with the aims of entertaining yourself, playing with your partner, and entertaining the audience. On Swipe Dating Apps, your goal is to create a playful conversation that entertains you and your match and makes them want to spend time with you. This is why just sending a message like "Hey" or "Hi" is not very effective.

If you were out at a bar or a party and saw someone you were attracted to, you could initiate with a simple "Hello," and a natural conversation may develop after. During a face-to-face interaction (especially in a social environment) that person will likely respond to you. They can react to not only your words but your voice tonality, facial expressions, gestures, and eye contact. However over Swipe Dating Apps, you are not afforded any of the luxuries of nonverbal communication.

You have only your words, and so you must use them effectively.

Fortunately, unlike in a face-to-face interaction, over Tinder you don't have the pressure of having to come up with something on the spot right away. There is no spotlight on you and there is no audience waiting in eager anticipation for your next move. You can take some time to write your message, and you should. You don't have to spend years writing and editing a novel, but you don't want to send a message with obvious spelling or grammatical errors. Just as you did with your profile design, you want to make a good first impression.

A good initiation in an opening improv set should set the tone of the scene while also giving the other person an easy way to react. If you can initiate with a strong emotion as well, even better. This should be the same goal for your first Swipe Dating App message. You want to set the tone of the conversation (playful, not overly serious) while also making it easy for your match to respond. Don't be overly cryptic and don't come out of the gates swinging with sarcasm (unless you read your match's bio, and they mentioned a love for sarcasm in which case they're probably fishing for it).

Now, usually a word from the audience will inspire an improv scene. On Swipe Dating Apps, your match's profile is your audience; their pictures and bio, your inspiration. Therefore, it is easier to start a conversation with someone who has a complete and interesting profile.

MY SECOND SWIPE DATING APP MESSAGING RULE THAT EVERYONE SHOULD FOLLOW

This rule applies to not only your first message, but every message after. You always want to *message with purpose.*

What do I mean? I mean:

> If you don't know why you are sending a
> message or don't know what idea you are
> conveying with your words,
> **DON'T SEND THAT MESSAGE.**

One more time with extra emphasis:

> # IF YOU DON'T KNOW WHY YOU ARE SENDING A MESSAGE OR DON'T KNOW WHAT IDEA YOU ARE CONVEYING WITH YOUR WORDS, *DON'T SEND THAT MESSAGE*.

Okay, don't yell this rule out loud, it's longer than the last one, and you'll probably strain your voice which you'll need for all the conversations you'll be having on the dates you'll be going on after reading this book.

Your words do carry weight though. I know it may be common sense but always think about the words you want to use before you say them or type them. Again, this is true on and off Swipe Dating Apps. When we say things without really feeling into what we're saying or thinking about what we're saying, we tend to get ourselves in trouble.

Take a breath before you speak. Take two if you want. In the case of Swipe Dating Apps, you can take several breaths before sending a message. Really feel into the intention of your message.

Now that we have breathed and feel centered, how can we use our words to start a conversation out of thin air with ease?

GET OUT YOUR METAPHORICAL FLASHLIGHT!

There is more than one way to skin a cat, but I wouldn't recommend skinning a cat at all; that's gross and cruel. Unless you happen to be trapped on a remote island somewhere inhabited only by cats, and they are your only source of food. In which case, I don't even know how you're reading this book right now.

I know there are countless ways to start a conversation with somebody; however, you want to start a conversation that *entertains* and *invites curiosity* and *interest*.

The easiest way to do this is to...

> **Identify something that stands out in your match's photos or bio and shine a light on it in a clever and/or interesting way.**

Here are some quick examples for inspiration:

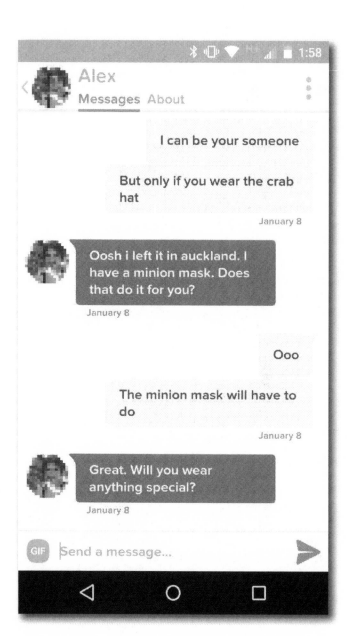

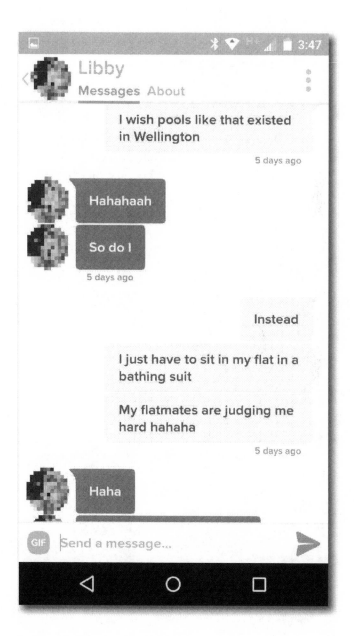

These were all opening messages I used in the past that led to first dates. The full conversations are available in Appendix 1 for you to read and analyze as well.

WHAT DO YOU MEAN "SOMETHING THAT STANDS OUT"?

You probably have a good idea from the examples, but again, I am not you. I don't know what you like or are into. I can't tell you what to write or say specifically. When you match with somebody, I'm sure you'll see something about them that stands out to you. The fact that you both matched with each other means you both at the very least find each other physically attractive and (hopefully) interesting in some other way.

The mutual physical attraction is a given, therefore it doesn't make sense to shine a light on someone's physical appearance unless the person is expressing themselves in a photo in a way that you find interesting.

Remember: you want to start a playful conversation that leads somewhere. If you make a boring statement about someone's appearance or ask a close-ended (yes/no) question the conversation will often stray right into a dead end. And we don't want that.

Examples of bad openers:
- "I like your eyes ☺"
- "Do you lyke my 6 pack?"
- "Dam gurl/boi, dat booty fine"
- W4nn4 b4nG 14ter?
- "Hi"
- "Etc."

HOW DO I "SHINE A LIGHT" IN A CLEVER AND/OR INTERESTING WAY?

Comment on something in a manner that...

1. *Demonstrates your knowledge or passion* of a subject you're interested in
2. *Provides a glimpse* into your personal philosophy on an idea
3. *Expresses how you feel* about something in their profile

You can pick one of these approaches or go all out and incorporate them all like I did right here:

In this example, I saw Jac was playing a C chord on a guitar in her profile picture. In my first message I demonstrated that I too am knowledgeable and passionate about playing guitar, informed her that the C chord is my favorite to play, and expressed that I love that she is also a musician.

She responded with her philosophy and how she feels about Tinder as well as a compliment on one of my photos which opened up the conversation right away.

You want to allow people to *feel* who you are right away. Give them a feeling to latch onto.

Your unique point of view is interesting enough to strangers. Remember: what's ordinary to you is often extraordinary to others!

Additionally, I prefer to open with a statement because it allows you to better steer the conversation, but sometimes I will open with a question if I am genuinely interested and curious about something in their profile. Just make sure to ask an open-ended question and don't fall into the trap of being the interviewer.

Here's an example of an open-ended question opener:

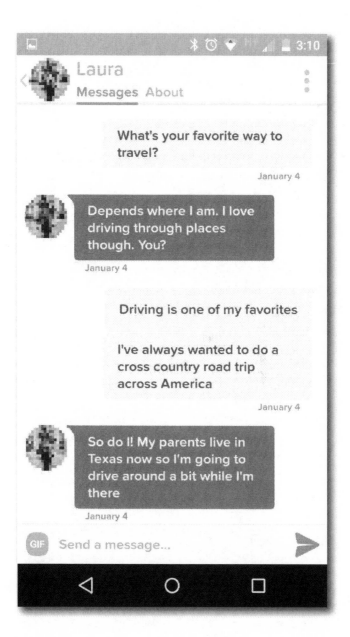

A good conversation should flow back and forth naturally and not feel too one-sided. Be genuine.

Below I've given witty names to a few of these examples and included a few more examples of effective openers that I have used. I call them "effective openers" because each of these led to a conversation that led to a date. Note that while I have titled them after-the-fact, none of these are canned lines. Each were written after viewing the full profile of a match, and you should do the same. The goal here is not for you to copy me, but to show you how to observantly go through a match's profile and craft a better first message.

THE "CREATE A SCENE" OPENER:

This is my favorite way to start a conversation. It's how to initiate a conversation like an improviser and create a conversational game right off the bat. To do this, the other person's profile has to have good, expressive photos. I was going through a profile once and saw my match had a picture where she was steering a boat and wearing a captain's hat.

I opened with "I see I've found a captain for my journey."

She responded saying she loved that she gets to be the captain.

The conversation turned into a fun back and forth about our "life at sea."

This continued until she commented on something in my profile and asked a question about that, and I brought the conversation "down to Earth" and made plans to meet up.

THE BETTER QUESTION OPENER:

I often run into profiles where the other person expresses an interest in travel. I used to live abroad, so this is a topic of interest for me as well. Instead of asking a boring question like "Where have you traveled to?" Instead ask them a more directed one like "What do you love most about traveling?" or "What's your favorite way to travel?"

I used this approach in my conversation with Laura which led to us talking about why we both love road trips.

If you do open with a question, ask a better question or one that's out of the ordinary.

How can you create a better question?

That's a great question ;)

In improvisation, we use something called A, B, C Thinking to generate ideas. We get a word from the audience like "boat" and then in our heads we go "A makes me think of B which makes me think of C." So for this example, boat makes me think of pirates which makes me think of treasure!

So if I was on a Dating App, I could ask a question like...

- "I see you have a boat, but are you a pirate? Which island should we ransack first?"
- "You must be a pirate, but are you going to share the treasure with me?"
- "Where did you learn to drive a boat? I've always wanted to learn!"

- "What's your favorite thing about being on the water?"
- "How are you going to fight the Kraken when you're on the water?"

These are just a few that I thought of after doing the A, B, C exercise. Some of them are also "Create a Scene" openers which is fine! The more creativity the better, but if you do decide to ask a question, make it a unique one!

THE SITUATIONAL WEATHER OPENER:

I started my Tinder conversation with Libby by saying "I wish pools like that existed in Wellington" after seeing a picture of her by a nice-looking swimming pool. At the time, it was summer and hot as hell out. I also knew very few people in Wellington that had swimming pools, so I used this knowledge to assume she was not from here (or if she was, I wanted to go swimming in that pool!).

I wouldn't advocate talking about the weather, but in this case it was a relatable initiation that led to a more playful interaction (and a date).

THE RELATED INTEREST OPENER:

This one's not complicated. Talk about an interest you have in common.

I love playing guitar, so when I matched with Jac and saw she was playing guitar in her profile picture, I commented on that.

As you saw in the screenshot above, I initiated by saying "I see you're playing a C chord. It's the best chord."

I love C chords because they're in the key of C which is easy for me to sing in (most of the songs I have written are in the key of C). This led to a conversation about music and eventually a date.

THE SIMPLE SHINE-A-LIGHT OPENER:

This one is even simpler than the last one.

One time I got a match, and in her profile, she said, "Bonus points if you have a dog, like craft beers or are outdoorsy and want to go on an adventure. ☺ " (Breadcrumb theory spotted out in the wild!)

I noticed in her photos she had a picture of a cute cat as well, so I messaged her saying "I like craft beers, and that cat on your lap by the ocean may be my spirit animal haha"

She responded and a fun, light-hearted back and forth conversation ensued.

Note: Again, these are my own words. You shouldn't copy and paste any of these lines. Every match you get will present new and different information, and you want to send a unique message in your own voice. Instead, look at these examples and try to adapt the mind of an improviser when crafting your messages.

Another Note: I would post screenshots of all of these conversations here, but the fact is I didn't save screenshots of them all. I have posted all the conversations I *do* have in Appendix 1 for you to read and analyze on your own.

> **ACTION:** A good way to exercise your observational muscle is to think or write down things you find interesting in people's profiles while swiping. What stands out to you besides their looks? Are they doing an activity that you also enjoy? You can also do this walking down the street or pretty much anywhere there are people. What stands out to you about the strangers you see? The more you exercise your observational muscle the easier it will be to craft first messages.

ALL POSSIBLE OUTCOMES OF INITIATING LIKE AN IMPROVISER:

When you send a message that shines a light on something in your match's profile, they can respond in only three ways:

1.   A "NO" RESPONSE

They don't respond at all. In an improv scene this could be disastrous. If you got a "no" response on stage or were negated for something you just said, you would be confused and not know what to do, you and your partner would look bad, and the audience would be confused as to what was actually happening.

On Tinder, the stakes are much lower though. There are plenty of reasons why a match could not respond to your message. Maybe they're too busy to take the time to message you back. Maybe they looked at your profile and decided they actually aren't that interested. Maybe they don't understand your humor, in which case, the date would probably not have gone well anyways.

Whatever the reason, you lose nothing, so keep swiping and messaging!

2.   A "YES" RESPONSE

They respond and agree with your statement but nothing more. In an improv scene, this isn't ideal, but it's not disastrous. It means you will have to work harder to make the scene work because your partner isn't fully playing along yet.

On Swipe Dating Apps, this means your match is interested in talking to you, but is not fully interested in the conversation. Again, you will have to work harder in the conversation to get them hooked and hopefully lead them to...

3.   A "YES, AND..." RESPONSE

This is the best response: The Holy Grail of Responses. Your match responds, agrees with your statement, and then adds something else to the conversation.

This is the response you should be getting if you send a message that shines a light on something in your match's profile in a clever and/or interesting way. By responding in this manner, your match has indicated that they are interested in you and are already contributing to the conversation. All you have to do now is keep the conversation going.

BUT WHAT IF I INITIATE IN A DIFFERENT WAY?

As I said earlier, there are countless ways to start a conversation. You *could* open with a cheesy pickup line (Damn girl, are you a beaver? Cuz dam) or a stale ice breaker (How much does a polar bear weigh? Enough to break the ice!) if you so desire... I think you have more creativity in you though! And everyone has heard those lines before.

The aim here is to start a genuine conversation that is at least somewhat original, unique, and entertaining for the both of you and also leads to a date.

And being genuine and authentic is the best way to do that.

If using canned lines *really* works for you, then by all means keep doing it and don't listen to my advice. In fact, if you're doing anything that's not stated in this book that's working for you, and not hurting anyone then by all means keep doing it.

I wrote this book for all the people out there who downloaded Tinder and other Swipe Dating Apps and still feel lost or confused. With that in mind, I hope this section helps you send better first messages that get more (and better) responses.

CHAPTER SUMMARY

Before sending your first message, keep these tips in mind:

1. If you wouldn't say it in real life **don't say it online**.
2. If you don't know why you are sending a message or don't know what message you are actually communicating with your words, **don't send that message**.
3. After you match with someone, look at your matches pictures and read their bio. Find something that **stands out** to you and **shine a light on it in a clever and/or interesting way**.
4. When writing your first message think about all the ways someone could actually possibly respond to it. If the response is limited to one word or yes/no, **TRY AGAIN**.
5. If you're still unsure what to write try to either **demonstrate your knowledge of or passion for** a subject you're both interested in, **provide a glimpse**

into a personal philosophy on an idea, or simply **express how you feel** about something in their profile.

If you've followed these tips and received a "yes, and..." response, then you are well on your way to creating a conversational game without even realizing it. The next chapter will examine games further and why they are important on Swipe Dating Apps (and real life) conversations.

Hint: Games are fun, and people like to have fun.

CHAPTER 3

PLAY THE CONVERSATIONAL GAME

*1. Identify → 2. Shine → **3. Play** → 4. Make Plans*

WHAT STANDS OUT IN A SWIPE DATING APP CONVERSATION?

We've now gone over how to send a first message that stands out on Swipe Dating Apps, and in doing so you should begin to receive more "yes, and…" responses. As we've talked about, a "yes, and…" response signals the start of a good conversation, but how can we continue the conversation in a way that is entertaining and also leads to a date?

Before we dive into the "how," let's look at the "what," specifically what men and women are looking for in interactions on Swipe Dating Apps. More importantly, I want to show why initiating a conversation online like an improviser works. You don't know me, many of you may not be all too familiar with improv, and at this point many of you are probably wondering, "Will this really work for me?" I know that anecdotal examples are not enough which is why I conducted an anonymous survey to find out what women (and other men) were looking for in their Swipe Dating App conversations.

In the survey, I asked a variety of questions analyzing different aspects of a standard Tinder conversation, but the most interesting question I asked was "What conversations stand out to you?" After analyzing the results, a few themes emerged. Let's take a look:

ANONYMOUS SURVEY HIGHLIGHTS:

Female: "Anything that starts with a **pun** usually goes well for me. Or a **get-to-know you game**. My now-boyfriend initiated conversation with "Two Truths and a Lie.""

Female: "**Witty banter** is always a good thing! And asking questions about each other makes it flow better. **Not delaying the 'date' too long** either."

Female: "Conversations that start **how you would speak to a friend** flow better. If men start asking breast size or weird sexual questions I usually don't respond."

Female: "I like people who **make jokes** about your photos or your descriptions. I'm pretty weird so it's nice when people stand out in that way."

Female: "Guys that use **unusual questions** or **"Would You Rather"** games tend to stick out because it's not the boring

'How are you? What do you do' routine. Had a guy who **played Truth or Dare**, which was interesting and fun and leaves the more routine questions for your (hopefully) first date so you're not stuck looking for things to talk about when you do meet in person."

Female: "The winning conversations are usually based on **witty banter** or **interesting anecdotes** about adventure/travel/unique experiences. They express his intelligence or leadership and sense of adventure/spontaneity, which I find very attractive."

Female: "The good ones are just conversations where we're both going **back and forth** with a good dose of **humor**, and it usually involves us both having the same interests"

Female: "What I've learned is that **people LOVE to talk about themselves**, online and off. It's nice when I'm made to feel like not only am I being asked about myself, but I'm receiving **thoughtful or funny responses**. My favorite messages with people on Tinder have included us **doing some sort of bit**."

Male: "**Good banter** always does better. If the girls show that they have a sense of humor and don't take themselves or the world too seriously. A little bit of sarcasm and irony goes a long way with me."

Male: "The good messages have a back and forth/teasing interaction. Doesn't matter if it's formal or not. The bad are the ones that feel one sided, and I'm only asking questions"

SURVEY CONCLUSION:
IT'S ALL ABOUT GOOD CONVERSATION AND HUMOR

At the start of a Swipe Dating Aeraction, all everyone wants is a **light, entertaining, and engaging conversation**. No one wants to feel like they are on a pedestal or being objectified, and nobody wants to feel like they're being interrogated. The conversation should flow naturally and not feel forced like when you're at a wedding and those relatives you kind of know but not really try to talk to you. And you can't escape because you feel obligated to talk to them. And then you excuse yourself to go to the bathroom, but you just walk over to the bar and order two more drinks instead.

Can't you tell I love weddings?

Great conversations are co-created when two people are actively interested in each other and contributing equally to the conversation. A great conversational tip which one of the women surveyed brought up is to talk to the person you've matched with the same way you would talk to *a good friend*.

When we do this, it's easier to feel more comfortable opening up and expressing ourselves. After all, we want to go on a fun date with someone, not sit in jury duty with them.

Humor or wit is also highly valued on Swipe Dating Apps (and in real life), and it's clear to see why: Everyone loves to laugh.

If you can make a stranger laugh, they'll feel more at ease around you and be more interested in you and what you have to say. The humor we use also provides a glimpse into our worldview and personality. Additionally, as one male survey respondent pointed out, a sense of humor shows you don't take yourself or the world too seriously which is an attractive quality.

We all have negativity in our lives and are aware of the negativity going on around us, but we're not actively looking for negativity in a one night stand/new friend/potential partner and certainly don't want to spread it to others ourselves. We all just want to be happy and find someone we enjoy spending time with; someone we can be ourselves around.

IT'S ALSO ALL ABOUT THE GAME

No, not the boring dating games like "You should wait 3 days to call him;" fun conversational games! Several survey participants brought up the topic of playing games or doing a bit together. Now you can play the more obvious games like "Truth or Dare" or "F*ck, Marry, Kill" or "Would You Rather…" but for several reasons I prefer to do a bit with my match or incorporate a game into the conversation.

When you play a more obvious game, it can become easy to get stuck in the game and lose track of the conversation. It's also not unique, so although you will learn about each other in a fun way, you won't be creating the type of connection you could be.

When you play a conversational game, or do a bit with someone, you are creating what is commonly known as an "inside joke." I'm sure you have inside jokes with your best friends. They are jokes that are only funny and make sense to the two of you.

Thus, inside jokes build a powerful connection between you and someone else and often are created organically between you and someone you are attracted to. Hence why initiating like an improviser on Swipe Dating Apps is so effective. If someone doesn't want to play along with your game, then they probably won't understand your sense of humor. If they don't understand your sense of humor, you probably won't enjoy spending time with them.

HOW TO PLAY A GAME

If you've shined a light on something in your match's profile in a clever or interesting way, you've already made an offer to play a game. It takes two to tango to maintain a good conversation and play a good game. If your match replies with a "yes, and…" response, they are already playing along with your game. To keep the conversation moving forward, keep playing the game you created.

WHEN TO PAUSE THE GAME AND MOVE THE CONVERSATION FORWARD

If your match asks you a question that's unrelated to the game, then the game has successfully served its purpose. At this point, don't keep playing the game; answer their question like a human being. When someone asks you about yourself, they are now investing in you. You already know they are physically attracted to you (they swiped right after all), and now you know they know how to have a fun conversation. At this point, if you keep playing the game and don't answer their question, they will lose interest and wonder why you messaged them in the first place.

An important rule in improv is to never let a scene drag on long enough that it becomes boring or stale. You can always come back to a good game in a new scene, and when you do, the audience will love you for it. Stand up comedians do this as well. It's called a *callback*. Every great comedian uses callbacks. They will make a joke that gets huge laughs in the beginning of their set and return to it later when you least expect it. In the same vein, you can always come back to a good conversational game you started in a conversation on an app, and if you can come back to it in person on a date with your match, all the better.

When your match asks you a question; it's a sign for you to begin your transition from playing the game to making plans. Don't dive right into making plans though. You are still having a two-sided conversation. Answer the question first, but when answering, keep the "breadcrumb theory" in mind from Chapter 1. Answer their question in a way that doesn't give away the full story but invites further intrigue and curiosity. If you do this right, you'll know exactly where to start the conversation on your first date.

BUT WHAT IF THERE IS NO "GAME" IN THE CONVERSATION?

Don't worry.

While playing a conversational game over Swipe Dating Apps is a sign that you may connect very well with your match in person, it's not required. If you and your match don't play a conversational game or create an inside joke, then at the very least, try to have a fun, light-hearted conversation that flows back and forth equally. There must be an equal back-and-forth between the two of you. If your conversations are drying up, try asking more interesting questions, or responding to theirs in a playful manner. Remember, you're not trying to get a job in an interview, you're trying to get a date online!

Also, as one female survey respondent pointed out, don't delay the 'date' for too long either. Good conversation over Swipe Dating Apps should only last for so long, and you want to make plans at the height of the conversation. Strike while the iron is hot!

So, once a connection has been established, make plans and meet up. Chapter 4 will examine how to seamlessly transition into making plans.

CHAPTER SUMMARY

1. If you've sent a first message that creates a game and your match plays along…**keep playing the game** until they ask you a question about yourself.

2. Even when not playing a game, **keep the conversation light-hearted.** Use humor and ask interesting questions to feed the conversational flames.

3. **Don't let the conversation go on for too long.** Strike while the iron is hot!

CHAPTER 4

MAKE PLANS AND GET OFF THE APP!

1. Identify → *2. Shine* → *3. Play* → ***4. Make Plans***

SWIPE DATING APPS, SALES, AND MAKING PLANS

Sales is a great metaphor for dating. As discussed in Chapter 1, think of yourself as a product. You have your own unique characteristics and benefits, and you believe in yourself (hopefully).

Believing in yourself is not enough though, you also must know how to sell yourself. Now I don't mean literally sell yourself. I mean you should be able to answer the question all matches will have in the back of their minds which is...

> **"Why should I invest *any* of my precious time in you?"**

If you've created a fun conversation with someone, then you've answered this question. You've *shown* them, not just *told* them.

In sales, a fun conversation means nothing if you can't close. Likewise, on Swipe Dating Apps, a fun conversation means nothing if it doesn't lead to you going out on a date with your match. I imagine you and your match don't want to swipe through pictures and send messages on your phone for the rest of eternity. You want to meet up with each other face-to-face and find out if you'd like to be more than pictures on a screen to each other.

In sales, you are taught to close at the emotional height of your pitch. You don't want to give potential buyers the time to doubt themselves and their decision. On Swipe Dating Apps, the stakes aren't as high. You're not signing someone up to a monthly monetary commitment; you're just making plans for a date.

The same principle applies though.

You want to make plans with someone at the emotional height of your online conversation when you're still relevant.

The height of your online conversation is *at the end* of a conversational game or, if you didn't play a game, after a few rounds of back and forth questions. This is the best time to make plans. You should have exchanged between **10-20 messages** at this point. If you don't make plans at this point, the conversation will either die out completely or become a tedious back-and-forth question and answer session that will cause the conversation to peter out into nothing.

Additionally, the more you give away online, the less you'll have to talk about on a date. You don't want an online conversation to become a first date because it can't. Ultimately if you want to connect with someone, you must meet up with them in person, and to meet up with someone in person, you must first make plans with them.

HOW TO MAKE PLANS LIKE AN ADULT

While the start of your Tinder conversation should be playful and almost childlike in nature, you don't want to make plans like a child. You want to make plans like an adult. This means the plans should flow naturally as a part of the conversation and should be specific.

Don't say "We should hang out sometime."

Or "Let's be friends."

I'm sure I said both phrases when I was a kid on a playground, and they worked then. We're not children on a playground anymore though, we are adults using Swipe Dating Apps. You want to make it as easy as possible for your match to meet up with you. To do this always be specific and always provide options.

Example of What Not to Do:

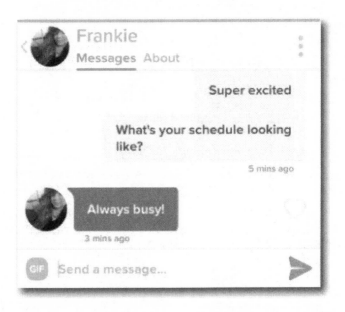

This exchange is bad from both sides. The initiator (totally not me...) is asking when his match is free but not being specific. His match answers with an even more vague response. If you're always busy, why are you even on Tinder?

Try to be specific if you can. If the days your match throw out, don't work for you, suggest days that do if you want to meet up with them.

When it comes to Swipe Dating Apps,

I always preferred to start with a coffee date. It's cheap for both parties and not too much of a commitment. If the conversation flows well over the app, I want to see if the conversation will flow just as well in person. If the date doesn't work out for whatever reason neither party has lost much time or money. If the date does go well though, I'll likely plan a more exciting activity with them for the second date.

We'll talk more about this in the next chapter.

To ask someone out on a coffee date, say something like, "Let's grab coffee this week. I'm free Xday or Yday afternoon."

It's always good to offer two separate days as we all have busy schedules. If your match is genuinely interested in meeting up with you, happens to be busy both days, (and is socially aware), they should offer another time that works for them. Logistically it also helps if you know a café that's convenient for the both of you.

Obviously, you don't have to go for coffee. You can go to a bar or restaurant or even play Whirlyball if you want! Again, don't limit your creativity and don't feel like you must do the same thing every time. Keep it fresh. As with sending your first message, read your match's bio, and if something sticks out, use that as inspiration for your date. Don't overcomplicate things though.

I once took a first date to the supermarket because in her bio, she mentioned she loved grapes. We bought grapes and walked along the waterfront of my city to a park where we hung out, tossed grapes into each other's mouths, and talked a while. Again, there's nothing groundbreaking here, I'm just paying attention to the little things.

Life is all about the little things.

Also, I don't know if this needs to be said, but I'm going to say it anyways: don't just invite someone over to your house. Even if the conversation is flowing well online, you should always meet up with someone in public first.

THE CHOOSE-YOUR-OWN-ADVENTURE DATE

Another way I used to like to ask a potential date out is to ask them a question like, "Are you more of a beer or wine girl?"

This allows me to better choose where we go while also getting input. I started doing this back when I was working door-to-door sales. When closing, we were told to always ask "Would credit card or direct debit work for you?"

The trick is you are asking a question but both answers lead to the same outcome. The difference is, on Swipe Dating Apps you are throwing out fun suggestions that leads to a date not a boring ongoing monthly donation.

You can use this technique with anything though:

Tacos or Chinese?

Waffles or Pancakes?

Horseback Riding or Skydiving?

Okay, maybe not that last one. Unless you happen to be *that* mythical adventure-seeking rockstar/brain surgeon we talked about in Chapter 1.

That was a callback.

Cue Laughter

I'll be here all night.

You get the idea. Feel free to get creative with it though.

HOW TO GET A BETTER IDEA OF WHAT YOUR MATCH IS LOOKING FOR WITHOUT DIRECTLY ASKING THEM

You can use the same strategy outlined above to get a better idea of what your match is looking for online if you ask something like "Shall we grab coffee or something stronger?"

Obviously, you can only make assumptions based off the answer, but I think at this point in the interaction, it's better than having a full-blown conversation over text about why you're on Swipe Dating Apps. It's also good to know what kind of date to prepare for: an afternoon coffee date, a happy hour drink, a wild night out?

As far as assumptions go, you can probably assume that someone who prefers to grab coffee is looking for something more long-term whereas someone who wants to grab drinks at a bar is probably looking for something more short-term.

Of course, there are exceptions, and at the end of the day an assumption is just an assumption.

Maybe they've just had a long day at work and would rather grab a drink? Maybe they don't drink at all. Maybe they don't like either and would rather drink tea. You can't know for sure what the other person is looking for unless you talk to them about it (and you should while on the date), but asking this question can give you a better idea of what to expect.

STAYING IN TOUCH OFFLINE

After making concrete plans with somebody on a Swipe Dating App, I would either ask for their number or leave my own. I personally preferred to leave my own and leave the ball in their court.

I did this for several reasons.

I realize that many are skeptical of strangers they meet online, and so I usually felt uncomfortable asking someone for their number. I also didn't want to appear overeager, needy, or desperate. If the person I was talking to was truly interested in me, they would text me or if they didn't feel comfortable texting me, they would continue talking to me through the app until they did.

Sometimes I didn't even have to do this though. Sometimes when I was making plans with a match, they would leave me their number without me even asking.

Again, as with the online conversation, don't overtext.

You cannot truly get to know somebody over a text message or a Swipe Dating App. These apps aren't designed for that anyways. There's a reason you can only talk to people who live near you. Leave the best conversation for the date. Remember to *message with purpose*. Text messaging at this point is a means to an end not a means within itself.

This is probably common sense, but if you've already made plans with somebody online, and you have given them your number or they have given you theirs, text them right away, so they can save your number. They'll probably put you in as "[Insert Your First Name] Tinder" because they don't know your last name. Or maybe if they're more creative they'll put you in as "[Insert Your First Name] Tortellini" or make up a last name for you based off of an inside joke you co-created.

You never know!

> **ACTION:** Give your dates a creative last name and then call them by that out on your first date! You'll probably create a great inside joke that you can call-back to at any time!

THE CASE FOR SNAPCHAT/INSTAGRAM/MESSENGER

Sometimes a match would ask me for my Snapchat or Instagram after we had moved the conversation over to text messaging. I think these apps are a fun way to keep in touch with your match before the first date and even more so after the first date if it goes well and you both hit it off. They allow you to give your match a glimpse into your day-to-day life.

Feel free to use these apps in addition to text messaging; however, making plans over Snapchat would be cumbersome, and I don't recommend it. You also don't have to use them at all if you don't want to. Consider them an optional bonus.

I use Facebook Messenger more than text messaging now amongst my friends and family, but I also understand how someone you just met might not want to share that information with you right away. Just feel it out, and use whatever is easiest for you.

Keep it simple. Don't overcomplicate any of this.

CONFIRMING BEFORE THE DATE

Back when I was single, I did prefer to communicate over text message than the Swipe Dating Apps' messaging interfaces because it was just easier. The Tinder app (and others) can be a bit finicky at times, and I didn't always have data or Wi-Fi especially when I was travelling abroad.

I'm sure others are in the same boat.

A few hours before the date, it's always a good idea to text your date to make sure they are still coming. This way you don't end up wasting your time sitting somewhere if they can't make it.

If something comes up well in advance of the date (you broke your leg, you have diarrhea, your cat ran away, you've won the lottery and are on your way to Cancun to celebrate, etc.), and you can't make it; **always message the other person**

and let them know. This tip is for everyone who uses Swipe Dating Apps and/or goes on dates.

It's just common courtesy.

Also, I don't know if this is common knowledge, but I feel like it should be.

If you are interested in seeing the other person and can't make the original date, it's *up to you* to let them know when you're free next. Don't create more guesswork for the other person, especially if they were the ones to make the original plans. It's easy to dismiss your match as a tiny picture on a screen, but they are a person just like you, and you should respect their time. Just as a good conversation should be 50/50, making plans with someone should be too. Don't make it feel like pulling teeth. A good relationship starts with an equal energy exchange.

I once went on a date with a girl two weeks after we originally made plans. We had to reschedule twice because she had hurt her knee. Every time she had to cancel, she apologized, said she was still interested and offered another time that worked for her. The third time was the charm, and we ended up having a great time!

CONCLUSION

Assuming you've texted the other person and they've confirmed that they can make it, you should be well on your way to your first date. In which case, stop reading this book and go enjoy your date! If you're still at home or on the bus or anywhere else and not currently en route to a date, feel free to keep reading. While this book is mostly about how to communicate better across the digital medium, the last two chapters will look at how to best transition from the online world to the real world for the date and beyond.

CHAPTER SUMMARY

1. **Make specific plans** on Tinder. Provide options. **Always** meet up in public first.

2. You *can* ask for your match's number, but I **prefer to leave mine** because if they are truly interested, *they will text you.* If they are interested but don't feel comfortable texting you yet, they will keep messaging you over the app until they are.

3. **Don't over text**. Leave the best conversation for the date.

4. **Always confirm before a date** or let the other person know if you can't make it. If you are the one cancelling, **offer another time** if you're still interested.

CHAPTER 5

THE FIRST DATE

PREPARING FOR YOUR DATE

If after all that swiping and typing, you've managed to create a fun conversation with somebody you're excited about meeting and then made plans with them, well congratulations, you're now using Swipe Dating Apps for their intended purpose: to go on more dates. If you've been on an online date before or any date for that matter, you probably have a good idea what to expect. If you haven't though, or if it's been awhile, you're probably feeling a little nervous and unsure of yourself.

Up until this point we've only talked about effective communication and expression over the digital medium, but these same communication techniques *can be and should be* used in real life as well. That was the point: to talk to somebody online like you would talk to somebody in real life.

The key is to remember everything we've talked about in this book so far...*and then forget it.*

The most important thing you can do in preparation for your date besides showering and making sure you look and feel your best is to **be present**. You want to be active in the conversation and listening, not thinking about what you're going to say next or what you ate for dinner last night or that deadline you have coming up next week at work. This is why if you're heading to a date, don't read this or any other dating advice, and don't be swiping on Tinder! That's just rude.

Just breathe and notice the world around you. You have everything you need to have a great conversation. Now make sure you're as present and aware as you can be.

HOW TO GREET YOUR DATE

You walk into a busy café or bar. You look at a picture of your match on your phone and scan the room. There are people all around enjoying their coffee or beer and chatting, but you can't seem to find your date.

What do you do?

Easy.

If the other person arrives before you, and you're in a loud environment, think like a hostess at a busy restaurant and shout out, "[Your Match's Name] from Tinder!?"

"[Insert Match's Name]!?!!?...from Tinder!?!??!?"

If there are enough people in the room, there will be somebody with your match's name who is also on Tinder who will gladly have a drink with you.

That was another joke, don't do that.

I once went up to a girl at a café and asked if she was the girl I was meeting from Tinder.

She was not.

It was a little awkward, but when I told my Tinder date about it, she thought it was hilarious; an honest mistake AND an easy ice breaker.

Realistically, you should be able to find your match by looking at their picture and looking around you. Unless of course your match looks nothing like their pictures in which case, get the hell out of there!

If you arrived before your match, text them and tell them you're the guy/girl leaning against the wall and hitting the jukebox looking cool (because most bars totally still have jukeboxes) or you're sitting at the table by the window writing haikus or picking your nose or whatever.

When you do finally see your date, make eye contact with them, smile, and greet them with a hug. I like to greet my dates with a hug because it invites familiarity. Treat them like they're your best friend, not just a stranger you met on the internet. If you greet them like you already know them and have hung out a bunch, they will feel more at ease and comfortable around you.

Emotions are contagious. If you feel awkward and nervous, so will your date. If you do feel awkward or nervous though, it's better to tell your date upfront and be honest about it. Don't just try to soldier through it. Here's why:

THE PERFORMER/AUDIENCE RELATIONSHIP, EMOTIONAL CONTAGION, AND DATES

Greeting your date for the first time is a lot like doing stand up comedy for the first time. If you've never done it before, it can seem terrifying, and you might want to throw up. If you have to throw up, do it before you're on stage (or in front of your date).

When you're doing standup or performing or presenting in any aspect, there exists a relationship between the audience and the performer/speaker. If a show has been branded as a comedy show, the audience has come and paid money to laugh, and they want to see you do well. This is why if you are new to comedy and come out on stage and are nervous; just be honest about it.

If you mess up a joke or stumble over your words, it's better to call yourself out on it. When you do this, the audience will empathize with you instead of sympathizing for you. You never want an audience to feel bad for you. When you call yourself out and are honest with the audience though, they will encourage you and applaud your efforts to do something that they are likely too scared to do themselves. You reveal the humanity in what you are doing, and the audience relates to that.

The audience will feel the emotions that you feel on stage, and a good performer will always be in control of their emotions and use them to their advantage. If they want the audience to feel upset at something, they will act upset. If they want the audience to feel excited, they will act excited. And so on.

While there are countless styles of comedy, most professional comedians you watch who are good at what they do, carry themselves on stage in a relaxed and composed manner. They know that if they are calm and collected, the audience will be as well, and when they finally deliver a punchline, the audience won't see it coming.

This emotional contagion between audience and performer is the same emotional contagion that exists between you and someone else when you're out on a date (or in a job interview or at a party or at work). If you've never been out on a date before you will likely feel nervous, just as I felt nervous the first time I ever did stand up comedy.

Again, this is fine; just remember to address the elephant in the room right off the bat. The more dates you go on though, the more comfortable you will feel, and the more comfortable you feel, the more comfortable your date will feel.

HOW TO START THE CONVERSATION: PART 1

After greeting your match with a hug and a "Hey there" or "Hi" or "Hello" or however you introduce yourself, continue the conversation like you just ran into your best friend on the street.

You'd probably ask them how their day was or their job or whatever it was you talked about earlier. This is a great time to drop in a callback to an earlier joke or bit you both had during your online conversation. At this point, you should be in line to get coffee or drinks. Keep the conversation light.

TO PAY FOR DRINKS OR NOT?

This is an issue that is commonly debated online in blogs and dating articles.

"Should the man pay for the first date?"

When it comes to whether you should pay for drinks or not, I'm going to leave that up to you.

I've been on dates where I've paid for the drinks, and I've also been on dates where we both paid for our own.

When I did have a stable job and income, I always at least offered to pay for the first round if it was just drinks. If you don't have a stable job and income, like I once did, I wouldn't recommend going out of your way to pay for everything... If a woman or guy is talking to you because they think you have money, the date is probably not going to work out anyways.

Unless the date was from SeekingArrangement.com and one of you is looking for a Sugar Daddy or a Sugar Momma. This book isn't about that though!

If you are at a bar, and have a stable income, and are still confused, pay for the first round, and have your date pay for the second. I find this to be fairer to both parties. After all, it is 2019, and most people have jobs and money and like their independence and won't likely be offended if you don't pay for everything. Honestly, don't overthink it.

Do whatever feels right for your economic circumstances, but don't let your lack of money (or whatever it may be) get in the way of your mojo.

HOW TO START THE CONVERSATION: PART 2

Now you both have ordered your drinks, and you've sat down. I hope you've been talking this entire time about anything and not standing in awkward silence. The conversation at this point doesn't matter a whole lot. You could be talking about how much you love this coffee shop or listening to your date talk about their day or their job or classes. Talk about anything at this point except yourself.

Again, keep it light. Your conversation in person should (hypothetically) be better than your conversation online because you have the added bonuses of facial expressions, voice tonality, and physicality. Be expressive.

Now how can we turn this shallow small talk into meatier deep talk?

The answer lies in listening.

FOR BETTER CONVERSATION, LISTEN LIKE AN IMPROVISER

When you're creating an improv scene with a partner, it's imperative that you watch them and listen to what they say. You're making a scene up on the spot, and you have to work together. If you're not actively listening, and you're in your own head thinking of what you can do and say that will be hilarious or cool or different or whatever, you're going to completely miss out on opportunities to create an amazing scene.

The same theory applies to conversation on a date. When your date is talking with you, don't be thinking about what you're going to say next and **don't *ever*** cut them off to talk about yourself.

Never cut anyone off when they're talking to you.

That's rude. Don't be a Fox News anchor.

And if you're offended by that joke, stop watching the news and do literally anything else. And don't get offended by people making jokes about people you don't even know!

I'm getting side tracked. What were we talking about again?

LISTENING, MICHAEL. WE WERE TALKING ABOUT LISTENING.

That's right! Actively listen to your date. When you do this, you will inevitably find things that you relate to or can connect to. Remember: your goal is to see if you connect with this person. If you want to connect, you have to talk about things that are relevant to the both of you in some way, shape, or form.

If you are talking about an experience that isn't relevant to your date, always ask yourself, "Why am I sharing this information?" If you can come up with a theme or reason like: this was an exciting moment in my life or a scary moment or a surprising moment, then you can connect that experience back to your date. If you can't think of a good reason for why you are sharing that information, then share different information. If you tell a story about yourself, then ask your date if they've had an experience where they've felt the same.

They probably have.

We all have different interests and life experiences, but themes tend to emerge throughout that tie us together.

In the same vein, when someone is talking to you or sharing information with you, first and foremost be listening attentively, but always in the back of your mind ask yourself, "Why are they sharing this information with me?" The answer to that question will help you learn about the person you are talking to and their motivations. It will also give you an idea of where to lead the conversation.

IT'S OKAY TO BREAK THE GOLDEN RULE OF IMPROV

The Golden Rule of Improv is "Yes, and…" or in other words "Agree and add more information."

"Yes, and…" is a brilliant way to start a scene and a conversation from scratch, however, on a date don't feel obliged to respond with, "Yes, and…" to everything your date says. You are your own person with your own unique ideas, philosophies, and beliefs. If your date says something you disagree with, it's okay to say, "No." This doesn't mean you have to have an argument with them. You should definitely *not* have an argument with them, but you should be able to discuss your opinions honestly and calmly.

If you really want to fizz up the conversation, disagree with something on purpose, but in a playful manner, with a smile even. This is a great way to introduce playful tension to a conversation.

In this Politically Correct climate nowadays, it's more important than ever that we are able to talk about our disagreements and discourses with our dates, friends, coworkers, and strangers alike. Not everything is black and white. In fact, most things are somewhere in the middle, somewhere in the grey. Nothing is off limits if you know how to frame your conversation and stay grounded and calm and speak from a place of curiosity and neutrality.

A GREAT CONVERSATION SHOULD TANGENT

A great conversation should not be linear. If you're talking to someone in a coffee shop for an hour on a date, and the conversation has been great, by the end of that hour, you should be talking about something completely different than when you started. You should have a hard time even figuring out how you ended up where you did.

The conversation has no agenda beyond, "Let's learn about each other and have fun."

Conversation for the sake of conversation.

Think about when you talk to your best friend. You're never putting yourself under the spotlight to come up with something witty to say. You're just talking about whatever comes into your head. When your best friend comes to you with a story or a problem, you listen with all of your attention before commenting.

Again, if you've established an inside joke online, feel free to call back to that or play with that throughout the interaction. Don't overdo it but keep that air of playfulness. This isn't a job interview, it's a date.

ACTION: Call up one of your friends or brothers or sisters or parents right now (I'm sure you don't call them enough, and they'd love to hear from you!) and have a conversation with them where you actively listen.

After making pleasantries, ask a good question, and sit back and really listen to what they are telling you. Make a statement about something you thought was interesting after they are done and see if they keep talking about it. Try to tangent the conversation so you end far from where you started. Talk for at least 10-20 minutes before saying bye.

Repeat this as many times as you want. You'd be surprised how much the people in your life appreciate hearing from you. Who knows, maybe after doing this a few times, you'll build up the courage to call friends you haven't talked to in a while. You never know what they may be doing now, and how they could help you. Hell, you might end up reconnecting and dating someone just by doing this!

THE END OF THE DATE

The end of the date will vary depending on the nature of the date and the connection established between you and your date. For example, the end of an afternoon coffee date would be very different to the end of a wild night out or a happy hour.

Did the conversation flow as well as it did online?

Did you genuinely enjoy spending time with this person?

Are you as attracted to them as you were when you first saw their profile?

These are all important questions to ask yourself at the end of a date. It all comes back to what you both are looking for.

ARE YOU LOOKING FOR A ONE NIGHT STAND, A FRIEND, A FRIEND WITH BENEFITS, A RELATIONSHIP?

It's a great idea to talk about what you both are looking for during the date. The point of the first date is to see how and if you connect with this other person, but even if you do connect, it's important to know how you both want to use this new connection. Honesty is important in *any* relationship.

If you went out on an afternoon coffee date, and it went well, you should definitely make plans to see that person again while still in person. It's always easier to make plans with someone in person than over the phone, so if you like the other person (and you initiated the interaction), go ahead and take the initiative again and make plans with them in person. If you only talked for an hour or so in a café, give your date another warm hug before saying goodbye. I wouldn't go in for a kiss, unless you had a truly stimulating conversation and *really* felt it was right.

If you have drinks at night, and everything's going swell, and you're both *feeling it*, by all means, invite your date over. Don't be crude about it though. You're not a caveman (or cavewoman). This is another time where callbacks come in handy. For instance, I was once on a date at a bar down the street from me, and the conversation was going well. When it came time to leave, I asked her if she wanted to come over and eat peanut butter out of a jar. I remembered she said in her profile that she loved eating peanut butter out of a jar. She knew what I was communicating when I said that and came over.

And yes, we did actually eat peanut butter out of a jar.

Again, it's all about the little things.

CHAPTER SUMMARY

1. When you find your date, **greet them like you would greet your best friend**.

2. If you feel nervous, **address the elephant in the room**.

3. To go from small talk to deep talk, **listen and relate**.

4. If you've created an inside joke online, **call back to it** during the date. Callbacks are especially useful if you want to invite your date over or vice versa.

5. If you want a second date, **make plans in person** during or at the end of the date.

AFTER THE DATE

Following Up, Managing Expectations, and
Staying Motivated While Single

THE HARSH REALITY ABOUT DATES
THAT FEW TALK ABOUT

While you go into every date hoping for the best, the reality is that not all dates are created equal. Some dates just won't go as well as others. Sometimes you'll meet up with someone, and after an hour of conversation (or even less), find you don't connect at all. Sometimes this is in your control; sometimes this is outside of your control. If you are single and looking to connect with someone, you will have to go on a lot of dates.

If a date goes well, it is important that you follow up if you want to continue seeing this person you've enjoyed spending time with. It's also important to learn how to manage your expectations and your attitude, so you don't lose motivation.

Being single can become a grind if you let it. You can choose to view dating as a chore, or you can choose to view it as a transformative journey. This chapter will show you how.

FOLLOWING UP

The follow up to the date is important if you want to keep seeing the person you went out with. As discussed in the previous chapter, if you felt there was a connection between you two, and you enjoyed the time spent together, you should make plans for a second date while still in person. This way, you've already laid the groundwork for the next date, and you don't have to go through the more tedious back and forth of making plans online or over text again. Before sending a text about the second date though, you should always send a text saying you enjoyed the date. If they enjoyed it, they will text you back saying they enjoyed it as well.

If they didn't, they will likely not respond at all because few people want to go through the trouble of texting you back to say "THAT WAS THE WORST DATE EVER. NEVER TEXT ME AGAIN! YOU SMELL!"

You would definitely get the message after reading that, but nobody is going to be that brutally honest realistically.

The above scenario implies you went on a low-commitment coffee date. However if your first date ended up being a crazy night out or a happy hour turned into happy hours, or any other scenario that ended with you and your date physically escalating rather quickly and having sex, the follow up is even more important.

Again, the follow up comes back to the question of "What are you looking for from Swipe Dating Apps?" Depending on your answer to that question, the follow up will be different. Be honest with the other person about what you are looking for. If you both were looking for a quick hookup, then the follow up would probably be pretty minimal. You both got what you wanted, and that's that. If you both hooked up and decided it was so good you wanted to keep seeing each other casually, then the follow up may be a little more substantial. These scenarios both assume you're on the same page, but often this isn't the case.

If all you're looking for is casual sex, but the other person is looking for a long term relationship, it may be best to leave it at that. Honestly, it probably would have been better to know what you both wanted before having sex. I know in the excitement of the moment though, we tend to forget to communicate anything beyond our most immediate desires. Just know that sex can and will complicate things if you don't communicate with each other and are not honest about what you want from the beginning.

MANAGING EXPECTATIONS

The best way to date (and to live) is without expectations or at least with reasonable ones, especially when it comes to first dates. We all tend to have expectations, and while some are founded, others are not. If you walk into a coffee shop expecting to get a coffee, you probably will because that's the point of a coffee shop.

However, if you walk into a job interview, and you expect to get the job, you may get it, but you might not. This is not to say you should never expect the best; you should have confidence in yourself and your abilities but always be prepared for any outcome. Don't put all your eggs in one basket, so to speak. When you put the source of all your happiness on a future outcome that may or may not happen, you are gambling with your present well being.

These same expectations can hurt you in the online dating world. The most obvious area where you can be disappointed is physical appearance. It is easy to distort images online or digitally enhance them with apps like Photoshop. Sometimes people will use older pictures to make themselves look better. More often than not though, I don't run into this problem, and if the pictures are edited, it is usually pretty obvious. The bigger (and less talked about) challenge arises from having preconceived expectations about your date's personality.

If you paint an idea in your head of what you think this other person is like, you are setting yourself up for failure and disappointment if they are not as you imagined them to be. This is why it is important to not talk too much online before meeting up. You might really enjoy the person you're talking to online, but they could act completely different in real life.

If you spend weeks talking to someone online and meet up only to find you two don't get along, you will not only be disappointed that your expectations were not met, but you will regret that you invested so much time.

[Note: Many of the women I surveyed did express that they like to talk longer online before meeting up in person. From a personal safety point of view, I understand where they're coming from. However, for the reasons explained above, I like to meet up as soon as possible. This is why I almost always suggest a coffee date first. It's in the middle of the day, in public, and not a huge time commitment.]

The most extreme example I've experienced of someone's online persona being vastly different than their real life persona happened when I lived abroad. Over Tinder and text messaging, my date expressed herself effortlessly, but in person she was one of the most socially awkward individuals I have ever met.

Walking to the café with her, I tried three separate times to start a conversation, but each time she simply looked at me, looked down, and kept walking. Making conversation felt like pulling teeth, and I quickly realized that this was going to be a long date. She had been so expressive and easy to talk to over the app though. I learned during the date that she spent much of her time playing online video games, and this explained her comfort online and discomfort in person. I spend much of my time performing in front of audiences, and she told me my personality intimidated her. It was clear to both of us that we weren't a good match.

Lesson learned: you can only really get to know someone *by spending time with them in person.*

STAYING MOTIVATED IN THE LONG RUN

There are so many reasons why you can lose your motivation being single and especially on Swipe Dating Apps. If you're using Swipe Dating Apps effectively, you will go on more dates. As we discussed, no matter how much planning or thought you put into a date, sometimes it just won't work out. You can choose to blame the world and other people or yourself, or you can take an honest look at yourself and the situation as a whole and learn. This is the best way to stay motivated in the long run.

Dating in the technological age has also presented new problems that generations before us didn't have to face. This next section will examine a few of them.

LEARNING FROM BAD DATES

If you had a bad date, the first thing I would urge you to do is find the humor in it if you can. As a comedian, I think you can always find the humor in situations whether they're good or bad. More often than not, the best humor comes from the worst situations. Then ask yourself honestly, "Was this date bad because of you or the other person or both?"

I went on a date once where I showed up at the bar, ordered a pitcher of Sangria, only to realize I left my wallet at home. My date offered to pay for it, but I was stubborn and ran home instead to grab my wallet. At the time, I didn't think anything of it, but looking back, I realized this was a terrible thing to do.

She probably thought I showed up, took one look at her, and decided to not even come back. I did come back from my house with my wallet though, but the fact that I left her alone at the bar for another 20 minutes was not ideal to say the least.

We picked up the conversation where we left of though, and I felt like it went well. Then I made my second mistake: I took her to an open mic comedy night.

DON'T DO THIS ON A FIRST DATE UNLESS YOU LIKE DATING ON HARD MODE.

Unsurprisingly, the show was up and down. Her cell phone went off during the show as well, and we were sitting in the front row. It was raining that night, and her mom ended up picking her up (she was living at home at the time). I learned it was her mom who called her during the show which means at that point she had probably already texted her mom saying, "This date is shit. Help!!!" When we parted ways, I didn't even get a hug, and she said "See you around sometime…maybe."

She may as well have said "See you around **NEVER!**"

Walking home from that date though, I couldn't help but laugh at how comically bad it was. What I learned was you should never leave a date after you've arrived…even if you did leave your wallet at home. Better yet, don't leave your wallet at home in the first place. Also, don't bring a first date to an open mic comedy night.

Sometimes though there is nothing inherently wrong with a date; there's just no connection, and that's fine too. This is bound to happen with online dating, and I've had several dates like this. After such a date, you learn what you're not looking for, and every time you learn about what you *don't* want, you're one step closer to figuring out what you *do* want.

I'VE BEEN GHOSTED

If you don't know, being "ghosted" is when somebody you've been dating just stops talking to you out of the blue. They don't tell you why they stopped talking to you. They just cut all contact, and you never hear from them again. Being ghosted sucks no matter who you are. Unless you're a psychopath in which case, I totally understand why people are cutting off contact with you and not telling you why, and I don't have much sympathy for you.

I'm going to assume that most people reading this are not psychopaths though, and I understand why ghosting has become so popular. People would rather not respond to a message than directly tell someone they didn't enjoy spending time with them or tell them they don't want to see them again and then give a reason why.

I get it. Most of us spend our lives avoiding conflict and pain, and these types of conversations tend to be painful and feel like conflict.

That being said, I would always recommend being honest and upfront with the people you date. We're all human and sometimes the thought of "What happened?" or "What did I do?" can drive us crazy and keep us up at night.

If you ghost people, I would urge you to stop and try out a little honesty. With the amount of options available to us now, it's too easy to not respond to people we are no longer interested in. I think every time we do this though, we lose a little bit of our humanity. We're forgetting that the other person we're talking to is more than just a face on a screen or a number in our phones.

If you have been ghosted, I would urge you to not let it consume you and propose that the problem lies on the other end. I wish I had better advice than this, but if you're being ghosted there's not much else you can do...

Unless you want to hire a Private Detective to track this person down and ask them the hard questions and report back to you with the answers. Hey, that actually sounds like it would be a pretty good Reality TV Show: "Ghosted!"

HOW A GOOD FIRST DATE DOES NOT ALWAYS GUARANTEE A SECOND

I once went on a first date with a girl we'll call Francesca because that was her name. The date went well by all standards. We met up for cocktails, and the conversation was great. There was attraction. I felt a real connection. After cocktails, we ended up stopping at a supermarket and buying more drinks before coming back to my place. We talked and drank until around midnight when she said she had to leave because she had work early in the morning.

I walked her down to her car, and we had what I can only describe as an electrifying first kiss. After, I made plans with her for later that week to go see a comedy show (not an open mic this time; I had learned my lesson). I felt so excited. I felt like Charlie at the end of Charlie and the Chocolate Factory when Willy Wonka gives him the factory. Okay not that amazing, but it genuinely felt like the start of a good thing.

When the day of the show arrived I texted her to confirm that we were still going out. She responded saying, "Sorry, already have plans."

"What? How could this be?" I thought. We had that electrifying kiss! We made plans *in person* right after. We even stayed in touch throughout the week. When I inquired her further about this she responded saying, "I forgot. It happens."

This hurt. There is no way she could have forgotten AND made other plans. Looking back, the excitement of that kiss may have made me too over eager which is a sure fire attraction killer. Notwithstanding, had she just said after Sunday night, "Hey Michael, I had a great time with you Sunday night, but I'd like to leave it at that." I would have been disappointed, but it would've been better than her saying, "I forgot. It happens."

I don't care who you are; this is a terrible way to treat people. It's hurtful. I know with the amount of options available to us now, it's easy to dismiss people or ignore them completely, but I urge you to be honest and speak from your heart. It may be harder, but in the long run it's always better for both parties.

And for God's sake, please don't say, "I forgot. It happens."

Now I could have given up on dating altogether after this experience, but I didn't. While I was upset at first, I took my own advice, learned from the situation, and moved on. A few weeks later I went out on a date that went well, and my faith in humanity was restored. In the world of online and offline dating, you will sometimes go out with people who say one thing but actually mean something else. While it would be nice if everyone communicated better (and was just a nicer human being), it isn't always the case. As with ghosting, if something like this happens to you, I urge you to try and not take it personally and keep your feelings and expectations in check.

I know I could have been better about managing my feelings and expectations, and it's a lesson I had to learn the hard way.

WHEN TO TAKE A TINDER VACATION

One bad date or a string of bad dates can kill your motivation to continue dating. The idealist in me compels you to not give up, but the realist in me knows that sometimes you have to. Sometimes taking a "Tinder Vacation" and focusing on yourself is the best thing you can do.

I know it seems contradictory for someone writing a book about how to use Tinder and other Swipe Dating Apps to admit, but back when I was single I tended to delete Tinder off my phone every few months or so. The truth is, I think Tinder is a great tool to efficiently meet and connect with people; however, I also think that with this technology we can end up spending too much of our time and resources searching for that perfect someone that we neglect ourselves.

When we're pursuing our dreams, doing what we love, and focusing on bettering ourselves, we tend to find the kind of people we want to hang out with and be around. Therefore, I propose when Tinder or any other Swipe Dating App starts to feel like a grind, just stop.

Don't allow yourself to become cynical or stop going out or working on yourself, but stop going out of your way to find someone. If you don't find anyone in your time away from the apps, you can always redownload them when you feel ready. With all your experiences away from the apps, you'll know yourself better, feel refreshed, and be ready to dive back into the dating scene as a new man or woman.

CHAPTER SUMMARY

1. If your first date went well, **make plans** for a second in person, and send a message later saying you enjoyed it.

2. Have **realistic expectations** about your dates. Learn to become outcome independent.

3. **DON'T GHOST PEOPLE** if you can. Be a good person.

4. If you do get ghosted, **try not to dwell on it.** The problem likely lies on the other end, not with you.

5. If online dating begins to wear you down or just becomes another stressor in your life, **stop, and focus on yourself.**

CONCLUSION

Well, ladies and gentlemen, that's it. You now have everything you need to download Tinder or any other Swipe Dating App, make an interesting profile that people will want to match with, send the first message, build a conversation from scratch, go on a date, follow up, and stay motivated in the long run while single.

I hope you now understand how to *message with purpose* in real life and on your smartphone, and I hope you understand my message:

1. Dating both online and off is weird and complicated.
2. Having a structure for your communication helps.
3. Expressing yourself authentically helps.
4. Using comedy helps.
5. Loving yourself helps (a lot).

6. Nobody has all the answers though (including myself), and you know yourself better than anyone.
7. Listen to your inner guidance always and follow your passions.

If you do that, you'll have a better time dating and living.

Here are some additional takeaways I want to leave you with from all the research I've done and experience I've gained through writing this book.

COMMUNICATION, HONESTY, AND MODERATION ARE VITAL

Tinder and other Swipe Dating Apps have made dating easier, but in some ways dating seems more complicated now than ever before. Although we can communicate faster and easier, that doesn't mean we should lower the quality of our communication. We should harness this technology, express ourselves and be honest and open with each other. Let's do our best not to lose our humanity.

Everything should be used in moderation, especially Swipe Dating Apps. Much like Social Media, these apps are designed to be addictive. I don't want you spending all your time on these apps, I want you to live a balanced life going on more dates. As talked about in Chapter 6, if finding someone is the only thing you're focusing on, and Swipe Dating Apps are the only way you're going about it, you can become discouraged. Have hobbies. Pursue your passions. Don't search for someone to "complete" you. The more you love yourself and your life, the more others will love you and want to be around you.

There's also a good chance you will find someone amazing pursuing your hobbies and passions.

SWIPE DATING APPS AS A CLASSROOM FOR COMMUNICATION

The more you use Swipe Dating Apps, the more you will learn if you choose to.

Using the apps can be an effective way to learn how to communicate and socialize over the digital medium and in person. The more successful text conversations you have over Swipe Dating Apps, the more dates you will go on. If you go on more dates, you will have more face-to-face conversations. At worst, a date will not lead to a second. At best, it will lead to a second, or a hookup, or a new friend, or maybe even a job. If you are someone who doesn't have much social experience, Tinder and other apps like it provide wonderful opportunities to practice and improve your social skills.

I think Swipe Dating Apps can also be great for people who just got out of a long-term relationship and may feel intimidated at the traditional prospect of "going out."

I strongly believe every experience in life, good or bad, is an opportunity for you to learn about yourself and grow. In the case of Swipe Dating Apps, you may find out what you want (and don't want) out of dating and a potential partner. On the other hand, you could meet someone who you connect with and genuinely enjoy spending time with.

I talked to countless friends and many people surveyed for this book who have met their current girlfriend/boyfriend/husband/wife/partner off Tinder and other dating apps. You never know who you're going to go out with, how you're going to connect, and what your relationship could evolve into.

IT'S A TWO-WAY STREET

We all have to do our part to communicate better. Men and women. If everyone on Swipe Dating Apps (and in real life) expressed themselves better and talked to each other authentically; I believe the whole Online Dating community would benefit. The problem is there is still some stigma around Swipe Dating Apps, specifically Tinder. Some view it as a legitimate dating app, while others still dismisses it as nothing but a hookup app. Ultimately, how you use the apps is up to you, but I hope after reading this book you at least consider giving them a shot. I also hope you don't become another Creepy Matt.

There's also other apps out there now like Shapr which use the design of Tinder but are solely for networking instead of dating, so do your own research as well.

Remember: what works for me may not work for you. I am a man, so if you are a woman who read this book, obviously not all of the advice may be applicable. Even if you are a man, your personality may be far different from mine. I do thin, no matter who you are, a little bit of humor goes a long way. I cannot force people to change the way they communicate though. As Morpheus told Neo in the Matrix, "I can only show you the door, but you have to walk through it."

I guess in this case it's more like, "I can only show you the apps, but you have to swipe through them."

This book was the result of my years of trial and error on Tinder and other Swipe Dating Apps combined with my experiences working in sales and performing improvisation and stand up comedy to provide relevant analogies and lessons. I set out to address the problems I encountered when I started using Tinder and the challenges other users still encounter today.

I sincerely hope this book provides clarity for many.

I also want to echo what Aziz Ansari concluded in his book *Modern Romance* (which I highly recommend for anyone looking for a more in-depth study on modern dating in the technological age).

Aziz said, "Everyone is dealing with the same nonsense. Everyone is on this boat together, and it would probably be good if we were a little nicer on that boat."

Let's do our best to communicate better together.

DON'T BE AFRAID TO BE CREATIVE; EMBRACE YOUR WEIRDNESS!

Finally, live your life with more creativity! In regards to Swipe Dating Apps, of course send messages that stand out and keep the conversation light and fun. You can do this in other areas of your life as well. Surprise your coworkers, roommates, and friends with a new and different way to say hello and see how they respond. Use the examples in this book as inspiration or discover your own.

Be the joy and the fun that you seek in the world.

I find it's sometimes easy for me to get stuck in my routines and sucked into the mundanity of modern life. When we engage our creativity though, we can make even the most boring moments fun and exciting. We can shine our light onto the black and white and even inspire others to do the same.

I also think when we express our creativity, often it's weird because we're weird. We are not the perfectly groomed, photoshopped actors who we see on billboards and in commercials, and I also believe that's not who we are attracted to deep down. I believe we're all looking for someone as weird as we are, someone who understands our humor, cheers on our success, empathizes with our failures, and helps us learn and grow as a human being.

We all have our quirks. When we embrace our weirdness, instead of shunning it, we give ourselves (and others) permission to express our true selves, and maybe if we all expressed our authenticity a bit more we would find our soulmates a little quicker? At the very least, I think it would make this world a more exciting and interesting place to live.

• • •

I wish you the best of luck with your search both online and off, and if you have any questions about anything in the book, feedback, praise, or criticism, I'd love to read your message, whatever the purpose! You can reach me at michael@michaelboothbycreative.com

If you liked the book and found it valuable, I'd love for you to leave an authentic review on Amazon to let others know.

Please recommend it to your single friends too!

If you're feeling especially generous, you can even buy them a copy ;)

If you would like a guide to help you with this whole swipe dating thing, I also offer coaching. I will work with you one-on-one to help you better express your authentic self, so you go on more dates. I hope to also make you feel better about the whole dating process in general.

Set up your complimentary session today.[12]

I also host a Facebook Live show called "The Michael Boothby Show" where I interview friends and strangers who are doing interesting things, pursuing their dreams, and exploring their creativity.

It airs Live at 7PM Central Time. Sometimes.

You can like and follow me at facebook.com/michaelboothbycreative for updates.

---

12 https://calendly.com/michaelboothbycreative/15min

I wish you much abundance and joy and hope to connect with you sometime soon.

Much Love,

Michael Boothby

THE GOOD, THE BAD, AND THE UGLY

Okay, this is the juicy part of the book where I promised I'd post a few of my Swipe Dating App conversations as well as a few conversations that others have sent to me. As you can probably tell from the title, these conversations range from good to bad to downright ugly. Feel free to go through and read them at your leisure and study them. You will also probably have a range of conversations in your Swipe Dating App Journey, but I hope after reading this book more of them are good and less are bad and ugly.

-Michael

THE GOOD

ALEX

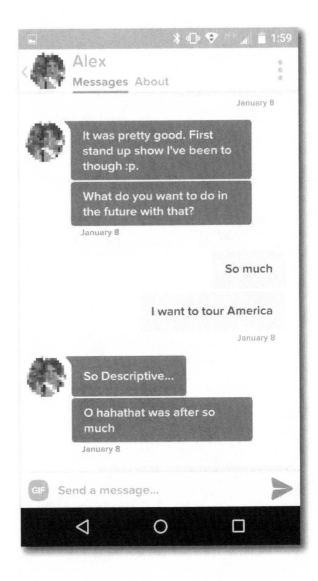

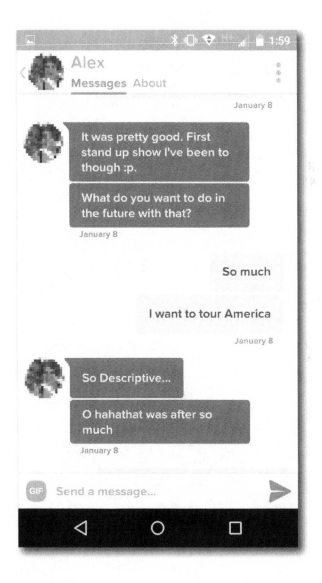

Alex
Messages About

Produce, write, and produce
my own Netflix show

January 8

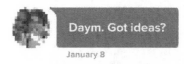

Daym. Got ideas?

January 8

Do motivational speaking/
team building seminars

Oh yeah.

I can't share them

But you'll see it soon if all
goes to plan

January 8

Haha fingers crossed:p.
Have you submitted it and
all ?

GIF Send a message...

Alex
Messages About

It's a work in progress. My writing partner is getting back in town this week

So we're gonna bang out a pilot and then look to cast

January 9

Damn thats awesome. Will be super fun too probably.

Sorry ima crash, but chat tomorrow?

January 9

Text me: ███████████

January 9

So when are you free for cocktail/beer/costume night?

January 9

 Send a message... ➤

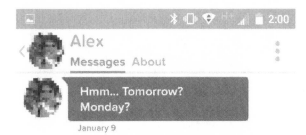

Hmm... Tomorrow? Monday?

January 9

I could do tomorrow night. 8 o clock at the Library?

January 9

Yep sounds good. Can i confirm tomorrow?

January 9

Yeah just let me know in the afternoon

January 9

So what are you up to tonight?

January 9

Meeting up with a friend to finish writing the format for

 Alex
Messages About

January 9

 So what are you up to tonight?

January 9

Meeting up with a friend to finish writing the format for this improv musical I'm producing

Then going out to dinner with some comedians

Then going to a comedy show

January 9

 Wow solid plan. Im going to botanical gardens for the music festival thing. Wait up ill just text you, leaving wifi.

January 9

 Send a message...

CARO

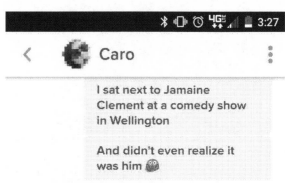

I sat next to Jamaine Clement at a comedy show in Wellington

And didn't even realize it was him 👻

3 hours ago

GAH!! Really? It was my dream to see them live since high school and I finally saw them in millennium park it was perfect

Caro 1 hour ago

Really, really. Oh man, that's amazing! I'm sad I missed them.

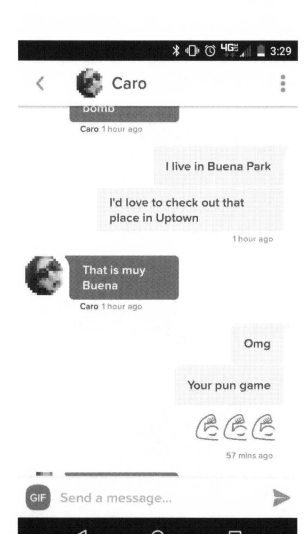

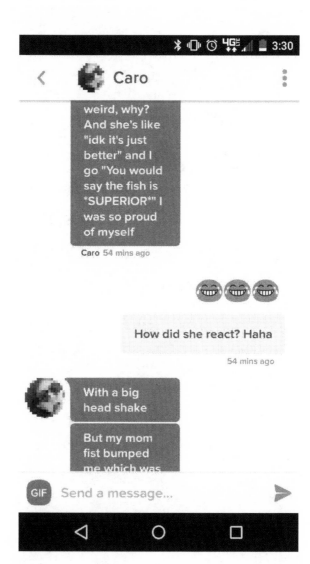

But my mom fist bumped me which was both awkward and life affirming

Hahah

Caro 54 mins ago

Hahaha that's amazing

Oh man

Do you wanna get Dim Sum on Sunday?

You seem awesome

53 mins ago

Send a message...

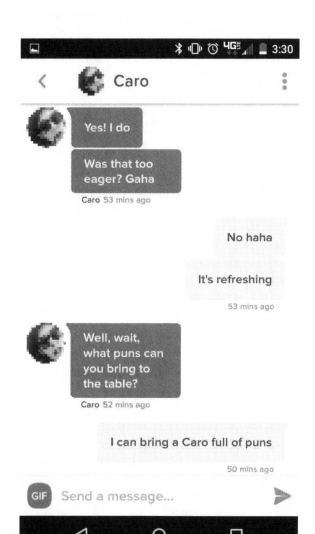

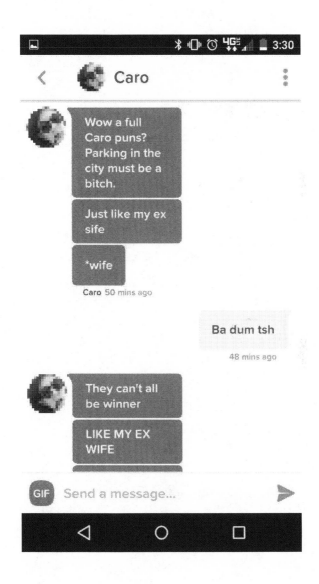

ELIZABETH

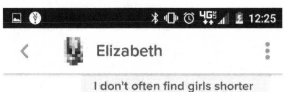

I don't often find girls shorter than myself

5 days ago

I often don't find guys taller than me!

Elizabeth 5 days ago

Well this appears to be a perfect match then

5 days ago

Ultimate dream come true
Haha

Elizabeth 5 days ago

You don't happen to enjoy music too!?

5 days ago

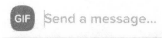

GIF Send a message...

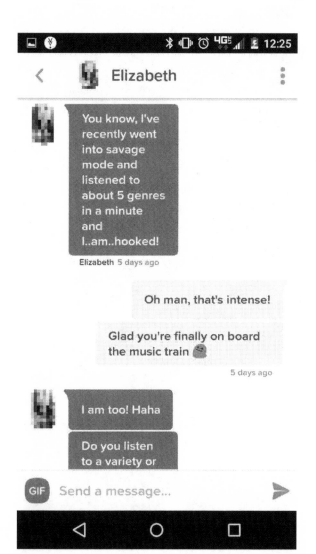

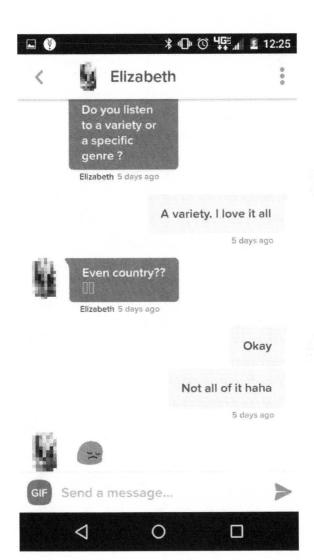

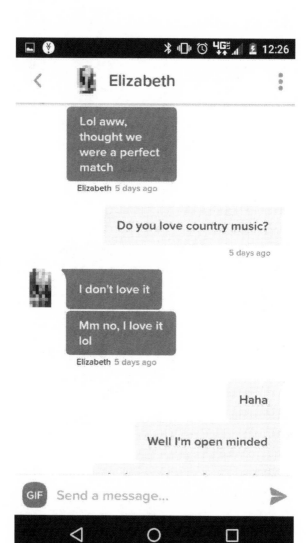

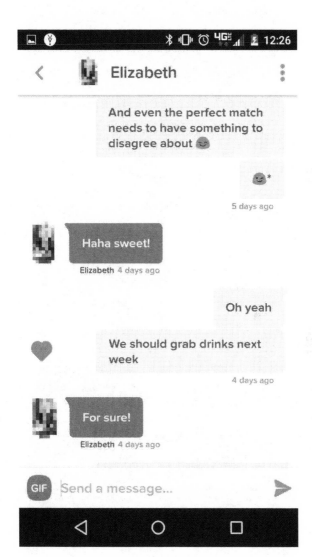

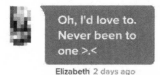

I'm going to a standup show Tuesday night if you'd care to join

3 days ago

Oh, I'd love to. Never been to one >.<

Elizabeth 2 days ago

Sweet!

It's at ████ ████████ ███
████████

Show starts at 9:30, but how about we meet at 8 for drinks and conversation first?

2 days ago

For sure (:

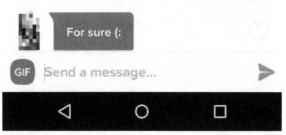

GIF Send a message...

ERICA

I live by Mt Vic and have always wanted to mountain bike it

I unfortunately do not own a mountain bike

December 27, 2015

 Ha take a walk m8! I ONLY talk to boys who own mountain bikes, you're just not worthy.

December 27, 2015

Ha. Oh man. I do run up it every day, but biking down it would be heaps of fun

December 27, 2015

 Tbh I wasn't planning on doing any mountain biking per se, just biking around

Send a message...

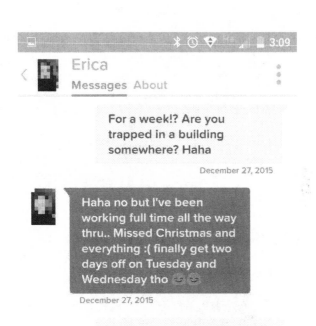

For a week!? Are you trapped in a building somewhere? Haha

December 27, 2015

Haha no but I've been working full time all the way thru.. Missed Christmas and everything :(finally get two days off on Tuesday and Wednesday tho

December 27, 2015

Aww well that's good! Where do you work?

December 27, 2015

I work at Spark 111 as an emergency operator, so like processing emergency phone calls what about you?

December 27, 2015

That sounds like a stressful as job

I'm a field campaigner for Amnesty International

December 27, 2015

Oh that's cool! I used to lead AI at my high school back in the day haha. What's the main campaign at the moment?

December 27, 2015

Nice! We're campaigning to end domestic violence against women in Papa New Guinea

December 27, 2015

That's a good one. So are

 Send a message...

Erica

Messages About

That's a good one. So are you one of the dudes that has to approach people on the street?

December 27, 2015

Yeah. If can be a brutal job haha

December 27, 2015

I always feel so sorry for them :(people are so rude. I always stop and chat! :)

December 27, 2015

People like you make our day! :)

You learn how to take rejection not personally. Because you face a lot haha

December 27, 2015

 Send a message...

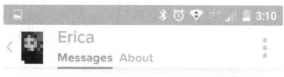

Erica
Messages About

December 27, 2015

Especially when the cause is so important and like, nobody cares. Too busy with their lattes and their gossip to care about thousands of women being killed every year lol.

December 27, 2015

Yeah. Def makes you super cynical

December 27, 2015

I can imagine.

December 27, 2015

You free Tuesday night?

December 27, 2015

GIF Send a message...

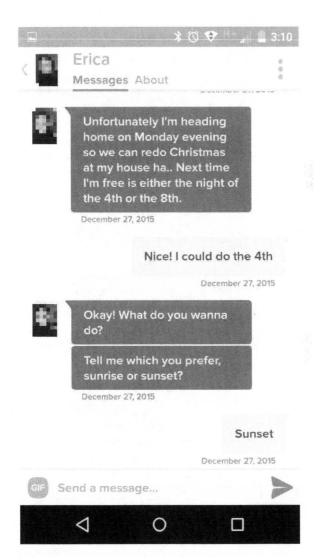

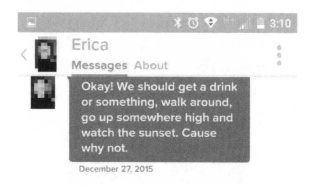

Erica

Messages About

Okay! We should get a drink or something, walk around, go up somewhere high and watch the sunset. Cause why not.

December 27, 2015

That sounds like a plan! We could go up Mount Vic

December 27, 2015

I was just thinking that. I haven't watched a sunset in a very long time, I really only see sunrises. Hopefully the weather is nice :)

December 27, 2015

Yeah, that'd be sweet! There's a dairy right under my flat, so we could grab some drinks, put them in a backpack and hike up

Send a message...

Erica

Messages About

Yeah, that'd be sweet!
There's a dairy right under
my flat, so we could grab
some drinks, put them in a
backpack and hike up

December 27, 2015

 Sounds like a solid plan 😊

December 27, 2015

Sweet! I'm not sure if I start
work again on the 4th or the
5th, but I'll let you know

Here's my number:

December 27, 2015

 Cool beans, I'll text u now
so you have mine.

December 27, 2015

Send a message...

JAC

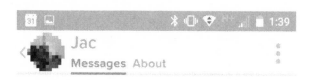

Jac
Messages   About

Looks like you're shredding a mean C chord there

It's the best chord

February 22

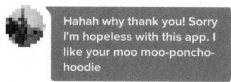

Hahah why thank you! Sorry I'm hopeless with this app. I like your moo moo-poncho-hoodie

February 22

Haha no worries ▮▮ ▮▮ ▮ks! There's a story b▮▮ ▮▮ ▮▮ ▮t moo moo poncho-hoodie

It involves comedy, nudity, and potentially hallucinogenic drug use

February 22

GIF   Send a message...

Jac

Messages About

February 22

It seems you don't check this app often, but if/when you do, I'd love to tell you this tale and hear a few of yours over coffee this week

February 22

 Haha, shortest tinder chat ever, I like it! I'm free Thursday around 12?

February 22

I can do Thursday around 12. Midnight Espresso work for you?

February 22

 Sure! Sounds good to me. I'll see you there!

February 22

Send a message...

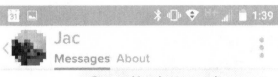

Sweet. Here's my number:

February 22

 Hey, are you actually possibly free tomorrow around the same time instead? Gunna have to go into work early on Thursday now!

February 23

Yeah, tomorrow should work for me

February 23

 Okay sweet! Is it really weird that we're meeting up when we don't know anything about each other? this tinder thing kinda overwhelms me I'm not sure why I'm on here haha

 Send a message...

February 23

Haha. It can seem overwhelming. Is it weird? I don't think so. I think Tinder provides an easier way for people to meet up and possibly connect

I'm actually writing a book about communication across Tinder that aims to answer questions like this more completely, so I'd love to hear your thoughts

February 23

 Haha, is that what your tinderology comment is related to?

February 23

Yup haha

 Send a message...

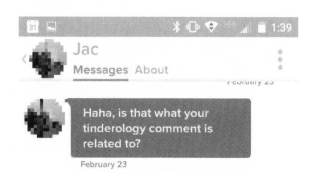

Haha, is that what your tinderology comment is related to?

February 23

Yup haha

February 23

Okay sure yeah let's chat about it. I have a lot to say about tinder haha and I'm sure you have even more to say about it so tomorrow will be interesting. Midnight espresso at 12 then?

February 23

Put it in my calendar. See ya there!

February 23

JENNIFER

Jennifer
Messages About

> New to Welly? There's so much to see
>
> February 28

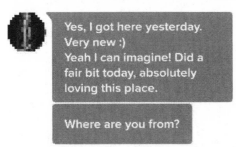

Yes, I got here yesterday. Very new :)
Yeah I can imagine! Did a fair bit today, absolutely loving this place.

Where are you from?

February 28

> It's a magical city
>
> I'm from Florida. Been living in Welly about 5 months now though
>
> February 28

Ahh cool! Working or

Send a message...

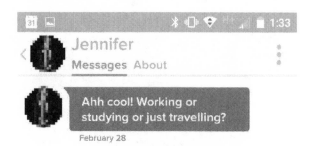

 Ahh cool! Working or studying or just travelling?

February 28

Working, performing, and producing!

What brought you here? Besides the wind

February 28

That's awesome! What kind of music are you performing and producing? Lol, well I have some friends from here and everyone says Wellington is amazing. and I didn't want to go to Auckland so here I am :)

February 29

Jennifer
Messages About

Good call! Not music but improv comedy shows. One's a fast paced show with tons of games and audience participation. The other is an improvised musical. I guess that show will employ my musical abilities lol

February 29

 That's heaps cool! How did you get into that?

February 29

It's a long story that begins on a cruise ship in the Caribbean and ends here in NZ

Would love to tell you over coffee this week in exchange for a few stories of your own

February 29

 Send a message...

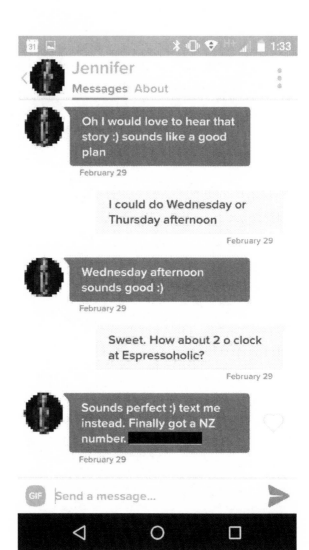

LAURA

What's your favorite way to travel?

January 4

 Depends where I am. I love driving through places though. You?

January 4

Driving is one of my favorites

I've always wanted to do a cross country road trip across America

January 4

 So do I! My parents live in Texas now so I'm going to drive around a bit while I'm there

January 4

Send a message...

Laura
Messages About

Are you also from the States?

January 4

No I'm originally from here,
I've just lived in a bunch of
places. You're from the US?

January 4

That's interesting. I am.

January 4

How did you end up here?

January 5

It's a long story

That begins on a cruise ship

January 5

Send a message...

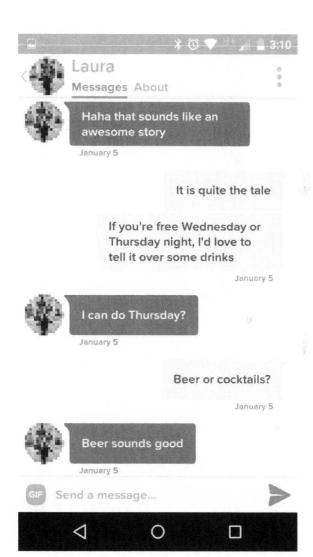

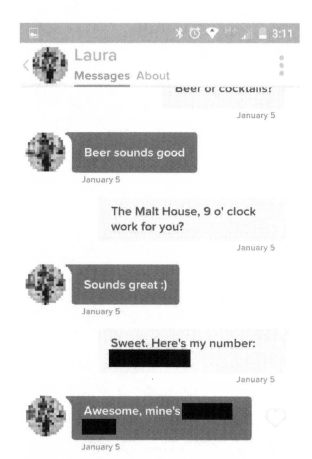

LIBBY

THE BAD

COLIN

← **Collin**   ⋮

May Fri 5 2017

I'm so fuckin in to some brunch

Mimosas or Bloody Marys?   ♡

Answer carefully   ♡

May Sat 6 2017

I... don't drink alcohol?

Delivered

Your message

Aa   📷   GIF   ➤

•   ⇌   ☐   ←

DAN

Dan

May Mon 22 2017

Hey there!

Hey Brooke ?

How are you today?

Just getting by at work wat r u up to

I'm on lunch. Just getting through the day. It's been a boring one so far

Tell me about it can't wait to get off

I like my job. It's a fun office. But it's never great to be bored.

Yea come save me

Your message

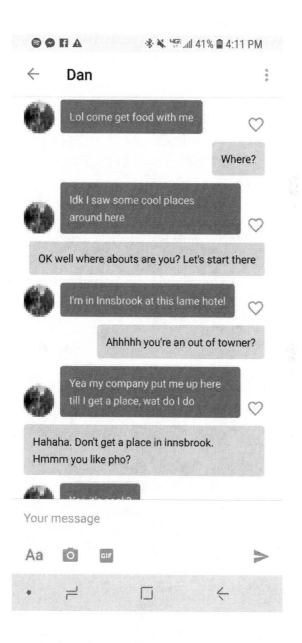

GIDEON

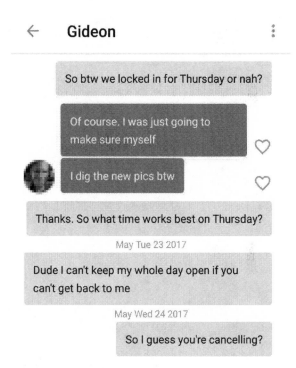

← **Gideon** ⋮

So btw we locked in for Thursday or nah?

Of course. I was just going to make sure myself ♡

I dig the new pics btw ♡

Thanks. So what time works best on Thursday?

May Tue 23 2017

Dude I can't keep my whole day open if you can't get back to me

May Wed 24 2017

So I guess you're cancelling?

THE UGLY

RYAN

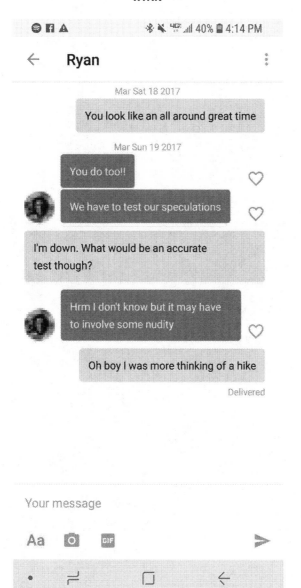

CREEPY MATT

 Matt
Messages About

 Fuuuuk hey sorry to start this way but youre incredibly fucking hot 😈

1 hour ago

You're allowed to start that way if you can bring it back to being normal

16 mins ago

 Whats normal

15 mins ago

Haha fair. I guess I just mean be willing to meet up and have a chat

15 mins ago

 What u looking for on here

14 mins ago

I don't promise or aim for

 Send a message...

Matt

Messages About

I don't promise or aim for anything. Just meet up and see what happens

11 mins ago

Well im looking for you to be my friend that gives me some benefit could that

9 mins ago

You can't just go straight to sex dude. If we don't get along I'm not going to fuck you

9 mins ago

I get that

8 mins ago

So we could meet up and see where this goes if you want

4 mins ago

 Send a message...

Matt
Messages About

4 mins ago

Tell me How do u like to be fucked

And i just have to say you do have a beautiful pair of x

3 mins ago

You don't seem to be understanding me

1 min ago

I do just tryna get to know u better

1 min ago

Getting to know me better is one thing. You're trying to get to fuck me quicker.

Ask a normal question

Now

 Send a message...

Matt

Messages About

8 hours ago

You don't seem to be understanding me

8 hours ago

I do just tryna get to know u better

8 hours ago

Getting to know me better is one thing. You're trying to get to fuck me quicker.

Ask a normal question

8 hours ago

What size is your bra and do u wear victoria secret?! They look amazing :))

Come on

8 hours ago

 Send a message...

THE ANONYMOUS SURVEY QUESTIONS AND ANSWERS

Q1

What city and country do you currently live in/most use Tinder in?

Chicago Illinois, America

Q2

I am a

Male

Q3

How often do you initiate conversations on Tinder?

Less Often (<50% of the time)

Q4

If you do initiate, how does the conversation usually flow? If it doesn't lead to a date, where does the conversation usually dry up?

I usually try and bring up hobbies/interests, especially if I saw something on their about me section that I'm also into/agree with. It usually ends pretty early, with a one of us saying something like 'that's cool' or the like, and the other just never responding again.

Q5

When you get messaged first: how does the conversation usually flow?

Usually a little better than if I respond first, but they still usually end the same way, just a longer convo.

Q6

Do any conversations stand out more than others? If so, why? For better or worse. Ideally, I'm looking for conversations that stand out in a good way but feel free to write about a bad experience as well.

I suppose they go better if one of us actually brings up actually meeting sooner rather than later. There was one time I matched with this one woman (turned out to be a dominatrix, though there's nothing wrong with that) that wanted me to meet up with her and her husband, I think based mostly on the fact that I was wearing a sailor moon t-shirt in one of my pics. The encounter was... weird, though I enjoyed it. To be fair, that conversation was just about sex, so I don't know if it's what you're looking for. Another good one was with this girl that I matched on tinder with. We talked for a while and talked about hanging out, but then she went silent. Didn't think much of it till weeks later when I'm at a karaoke bar. She messages me because she's there as well and wanted to see if it was me. This was a few weeks ago, and we've hung out a couple of times since.

Q7

How often do conversations that stand out (in a good way) lead to a date?

Once in a while

Q8

How easy or difficult do you find it to make plans with someone on Tinder? Do you ever experience frustration dealing with the logistics of the date?

Pretty difficult. When you're in your late twenties everyone has a job and friends and other things that they need to do, so logistics are a big problem. Though just getting to talking about hanging out can be difficult too. As a man I often worry about coming off as creepy/sexist.

Q9

Which factors attribute most to the success or failure of a Tinder Date? Describe in as much or as little detail as you want. [Success does not necessarily mean sex, but more did the date end leaving you wanting to see that person again? If so, why?]

Same as a date in any other form I think. We have things to talk about, there seems to be a mutual attraction, we're both having fun. Once you get past the tinder part it's all the same in my mind.

• • •

Q1

What city and country do you currently live in/most use Tinder in?

Chicago, USA

Q2

I am a

Male

Q3

How often do you initiate conversations on Tinder?

More Often (>50% of the time)

Q4

If you do initiate, how does the conversation usually flow? If it doesn't lead to a date, where does the conversation usually dry up?

The conversation usually ends when one of us wants to go to bed. Neither of us follows up in the morning.

Q5

When you get messaged first: how does the conversation usually flow?

I usually respond. I'm pretty good at keeping a conversation going.

Q6

Do any conversations stand out more than others? If so, why? For better or worse. Ideally, I'm looking for conversations that stand out in a good way but feel free to write about a bad experience as well.

The conversations that stand out are the ones where the other person talks in complete sentences and provides details that I can use to continue the conversation.

Q7

How often do conversations that stand out (in a good way) lead to a date?

Once in a while

Q8

How easy or difficult do you find it to make plans with someone on Tinder? Do you ever experience frustration dealing with the logistics of the date?

I've never personally have set up a date on Tinder. I have over Bumble and the logistics were fine.

Q9

Which factors attribute most to the success or failure of a Tinder Date? Describe in as much or as little detail as you want. [Success does not necessarily mean sex, but more did the date end leaving you wanting to see that person again? If so, why?]

Good conversation will make the date good. It helps if you find things that you are both interested in and talk about those. I would say success means you are both interested in seeing each other again.

• • •

Q1

What city and country do you currently live in/most use Tinder in?

Tampa, Florida

Q2

I am a

Female

Q3

How often do you initiate conversations on Tinder?

Less Often (<50% of the time)

Q4

If you do initiate, how does the conversation usually flow? If it doesn't lead to a date, where does the conversation usually dry up?

It usually flows pretty well until the guy starts to seem disinterested (i.e. messages less, short replies)

Q5

When you get messaged first: how does the conversation usually flow?

Depends on if the guy is more engaging and doesn't just want to find out what I'm wearing.

Q6

Do any conversations stand out more than others? If so, why? For better or worse. Ideally, I'm looking for conversations that stand out in a good way but feel free to write about a bad experience as well.

I had a really great conversation going with a guy I matched with back when I first signed up. We had a lot in common. We could ask each other meaningful questions and be playful. He was never off putting but seemed to be very honest. It was a nice balance. Unfortunately, by the time he asked for my number and then asked me to meet up, I had moved and we disconnected. But that was hands down my best experience on the app.

Q7

How often do conversations that stand out (in a good way) lead to a date?

Almost never

Q8

How easy or difficult do you find it to make plans with someone on Tinder? Do you ever experience frustration dealing with the logistics of the date?

It's easier when you've gotten to know each other a little better.

Q9

Which factors attribute most to the success or failure of a Tinder Date? Describe in as much or as little detail as you want. [Success does not necessarily mean sex, but more did the date end leaving you wanting to see that person again? If so, why?]

It's most successful when at least one person can break the ice and pick up the conversation from where you left off on the app. The less awkward, the better.

• • •

Q1

What city and country do you currently live in/most use Tinder in?

Los Angeles, CA

Q2

I am a

Female

Q3

How often do you initiate conversations on Tinder?

More Often (>50% of the time)

Q4

If you do initiate, how does the conversation usually flow? If it doesn't lead to a date, where does the conversation usually dry up?

when I start being weird

Q5

When you get messaged first: how does the conversation usually flow?

It is usually pretty boring and stagnant with zero chemistry

Q6

Do any conversations stand out more than others? If so, why? For better or worse. Ideally, I'm looking for conversations that stand out in a good way but feel free to write about a bad experience as well.

Conversations via text before meeting up?

One does in particular because it felt like we had a lot in common but we went on one date and he never called again, for whatever reason

Q7

How often do conversations that stand out (in a good way) lead to a date?

Sometimes

Q8

How easy or difficult do you find it to make plans with someone on Tinder? Do you ever experience frustration dealing with the logistics of the date?

It's been pretty easy so far, except recently nothing has been happening mostly because I'm not trying as much

Q9

Which factors attribute most to the success or failure of a Tinder Date? Describe in as much or as little detail as you want. [Success does not necessarily mean sex, but more did the date end leaving you wanting to see that person again? If so, why?]

I think it just comes down to raw chemistry and that je ne sais quoi type of attraction. And you can't really gauge that from a Tinder profile at all.

• • •

Q1

What city and country do you currently live in/most use Tinder in?

Chicago, U.S.

Q2

I am a

Male

Q3

How often do you initiate conversations on Tinder?

More Often (>50% of the time)

Q4

If you do initiate, how does the conversation usually flow? If it doesn't lead to a date, where does the conversation usually dry up?

I'd say about 50% of the time I just forget or find myself disinterested, 50% of the time they stop talking and thus probably did the same

Q5

When you get messaged first: how does the conversation usually flow?

USUALLY i'd say i do more talking. Women seem to get an overflow of messages so they're not really able to engage with any one conversation as easily online

Q6

Do any conversations stand out more than others? If so, why? For better or worse. Ideally, I'm looking for conversations that stand out in a good way but feel free to write about a bad experience as well.

The good ones are just conversations where we're both going back and forth with a good dose of humor, and it usually involves us both having the same interests

Q7

How often do conversations that stand out (in a good way) lead to a date?

Frequently

Q8

How easy or difficult do you find it to make plans with someone on Tinder? Do you ever experience frustration dealing with the logistics of the date?

When I was in the middle of it, it felt very difficult, but looking back, I probably went on at least one date every 2-3 weeks, which is about all I have time/money for.

Q9

Which factors attribute most to the success or failure of a Tinder Date? Describe in as much or as little detail as you want. [Success does not necessarily mean sex, but more did the date end leaving you wanting to see that person again? If so, why?]

Success: we both have a good sense of humor, the woman is intelligent, has good politics, isn't an asshole, has interesting things to say.

Failure: one of us just dropped out of the conversation, the woman was bigoted, etc. I had one date literally delete her account and not contact me the night of a date, so that was a failure. Had another date where the woman was absolutely wasted when I showed up.

• • •

Q1

What city and country do you currently live in/most use Tinder in?

Denver

Q2

I am a

Male

Q3

How often do you initiate conversations on Tinder?

Always (100% of the time)

Q4

If you do initiate, how does the conversation usually flow? If it doesn't lead to a date, where does the conversation usually dry up?

Convo is light and after awhile I'll ask them out for drinks. If they're engaged in the convo they mostly always say yes. This back and forth is only for a couple of hours after matching.it mainly dry up if she's not participating (asking questions). If that does happen and I'm still interested I'll ask them out the next day; worth a shot.

Q5

When you get messaged first: how does the conversation usually flow?

She's not real. And I get a spam message

Q6

Do any conversations stand out more than others? If so, why? For better or worse. Ideally, I'm looking for conversations that stand out in a good way but feel free to write about a bad experience as well.

The good messages have a back and forth/teasing interaction. Doesn't matter if its formal or not. The bad is when its one sided and I'm only asking questions

Q7

How often do conversations that stand out (in a good way) lead to a date?

Once in a while

Q8

How easy or difficult do you find it to make plans with someone on Tinder? Do you ever experience frustration dealing with the logistics of the date?

No...The only time is when they lag behind and don't tell me what part of town they live in. I also tend to give them a follow up "look toward to seeing you" message the night before the date that helps to relax my date. Or at least I think it does

Q9

Which factors attribute most to the success or failure of a Tinder Date? Describe in as much or as little detail as you want. [Success does not necessarily mean sex, but more did the date end leaving you wanting to see that person again? If so, why?]

Success = have fun + a second date. I do like to kiss but I'm not that aggressive. I'm looking more for future dates then one night stand

• • •

Q1

What city and country do you currently live in/most use Tinder in?

Sydney, Australia

Q2

I am a

Male

Q3

How often do you initiate conversations on Tinder?

More Often (>50% of the time)

Q4

If you do initiate, how does the conversation usually flow? If it doesn't lead to a date, where does the conversation usually dry up?

I depends on the chemistry right away. The conversation usually dies because the girl only answers my questions and doesn't ask anything back.

Q5

When you get messaged first: how does the conversation usually flow?

Girls who initiate conversations are usually better at asking things and help out to keep the messages flowing so it usually goes on for longer

Q6

Do any conversations stand out more than others? If so, why? For better or worse. Ideally, I'm looking for conversations that stand out in a good way but feel free to write about a bad experience as well.

Good banter always does better. If the girls show that they have humor and doesn't take them selves or the world too seriously. A little bit of sarcasm and irony goes a long way with me.

Q7

How often do conversations that stand out (in a good way) lead to a date?

Once in a while

Q8

How easy or difficult do you find it to make plans with someone on Tinder? Do you ever experience frustration dealing with the logistics of the date?

I guess I'm very impatient with chatting over the app. I always want to got for a meeting face to face as soon as possible and that becomes frustrating because most girls want to make an impression over the app first

Q9

Which factors attribute most to the success or failure of a Tinder Date? Describe in as much or as little detail as you want. [Success does not necessarily mean sex, but more did the date end leaving you wanting to see that person again? If so, why?]

Good banter and attraction is number one. If our senses of humor match and if you can have an interesting conversation and just don't get stuck in the "how are you, what do you do"-type of conversation

• • •

Q1

What city and country do you currently live in/most use Tinder in?

Brisbane

Q2

I am a

Female

Q3

How often do you initiate conversations on Tinder?

Sometimes (~50% of the time)

Q4

If you do initiate, how does the conversation usually flow? If it doesn't lead to a date, where does the conversation usually dry up?

Bit of humour. Sometimes I end up getting bored and I match or we meet up for a drink

Q5

When you get messaged first: how does the conversation usually flow?

If it's a cheesy pick up line I unmatch without writing back. Same with if I get called baby or hun. They don't know me yet so why use pet names. If it's a normal hello how you going then I write back and alway a bit of banta happens

Q6

Do any conversations stand out more than others? If so, why? For better or worse. Ideally, I'm looking for conversations that stand out in a good way but feel free to write about a bad experience as well.

No not that I can think of

Q7

How often do conversations that stand out (in a good way) lead to a date?

Sometimes

Q8

How easy or difficult do you find it to make plans with someone on Tinder? Do you ever experience frustration dealing with the logistics of the date?

It's very easy. Either they say or I do when are you free and the plan from there

• • •

Q1

What city and country do you currently live in/most use Tinder in?

Australia

Q2

I am a

Female

Q3

How often do you initiate conversations on Tinder?

Less Often (<50% of the time)

Q4

If you do initiate, how does the conversation usually flow? If it doesn't lead to a date, where does the conversation usually dry up?

Depends on the guy but a lot of guys were just interested in a hook up which I'm not so I would stop chatting! Sometimes we try to meet up and it doesn't happen so it may lead to an online friendship but only a small percent would lead to a date

Q5

When you get messaged first: how does the conversation usually flow?

It generally would flow well asking all the basic questions for example what do you do for work, where do you live etc

Q6

Do any conversations stand out more than others? If so, why? For better or worse. Ideally, I'm looking for conversations that stand out in a good way but feel free to write about a bad experience as well.

My favourite ones would be when they opened with a joke. I hated the ones where they just would say something like "your hot" or "I like your super girl costume" as it doesn't open you up to anything further

Q7

How often do conversations that stand out (in a good way) lead to a date?

Sometimes

Q8

How easy or difficult do you find it to make plans with someone on Tinder? Do you ever experience frustration dealing with the logistics of the date?

Generally pretty easy but I seemed to match with guys who weren't in the area which caused some problems. I also have a busy schedule so for a while there I was limited to only Sunday's for dates which doesn't always suit the other person

Q9

Which factors attribute most to the success or failure of a Tinder Date? Describe in as much or as little detail as you want. [Success does not necessarily mean sex, but more did the date end leaving you wanting to see that person again? If so, why?]

Conversation, physical attraction, sense of humour. If the date flowed well I'd be interested in a second date

• • •

Q1

What city and country do you currently live in/most use Tinder in?

U.S.A

Q2

I am a

Female

Q3

How often do you initiate conversations on Tinder?

Sometimes (~50% of the time)

Q4

If you do initiate, how does the conversation usually flow? If it doesn't lead to a date, where does the conversation usually dry up?

The conversation normally takes one of two turns: (1) the guy becomes vulgar/perverted/phonographically sexual (this is the most common turn), or (2) the conversation has general flow and last a couple of days before someone initiates the idea of meeting up (this has happened a handful of times).

Note: my pictures and bio are not sexual in any way.

Q5

When you get messaged first: how does the conversation usually flow?

Depends on their initiation tactic. Generally it will be a question/answer play till we hit a topic we can dive deeper into without prying through questions or the guy dives straight for the sexual in a less that respectful way and the conversation dies after I shut them down.

Q6

Do any conversations stand out more than others? If so, why? For better or worse. Ideally, I'm looking for conversations that stand out in a good way but feel free to write about a bad experience as well.

The winning conversations are usually based on witty banter or interesting anecdotes about adventure/travel/unique experiences. They express his intelligence or leadership and sense of adventure/spontaneity, which I find very attractive.

The conversations that are also memorable but awful generally involve ridiculous sexual assumptions or insults.

Q7

How often do conversations that stand out (in a good way) lead to a date?

Frequently

Q8

How easy or difficult do you find it to make plans with someone on Tinder? Do you ever experience frustration dealing with the logistics of the date?

Generally, the logistics is pretty easy to come up with and I have rarely experienced frustrations outside one of us running late/early.

Q9

Which factors attribute most to the success or failure of a Tinder Date? Describe in as much or as little detail as you want. [Success does not necessarily mean sex, but more did the date end leaving you wanting to see that person again? If so, why?]

Factors:

-Was the conversation interesting/intriguing?

-Was he respectful/gentleman like?

-Did he seem interested in me/my thoughts?

If the answer to those three was a "yes", then chances are I would be down for a second date, as I most likely had a good time on the first one.

If even one of these is a "no", I would be hard pressed to want to meet him again or even keep up the viral friendship

• • •

Q1

What city and country do you currently live in/most use Tinder in?

Orlando

Q2

I am a

Female

Q3

How often do you initiate conversations on Tinder?

Never

Q4

If you do initiate, how does the conversation usually flow? If it doesn't lead to a date, where does the conversation usually dry up?

I dont initiate.

Q5

When you get messaged first: how does the conversation usually flow?

Pretty well! Cheesy pick up lines that are exceptionally witty are appreciated. Sleazy comments get shot down very quickly.

Q6

Do any conversations stand out more than others? If so, why? For better or worse. Ideally, I'm looking for conversations that stand out in a good way but feel free to write about a bad experience as well.

Good conversations about history always stand out. Or exceptionally witty ones. Witty banter is much appreciated.

Q7

How often do conversations that stand out (in a good way) lead to a date?

Once in a while

Q8

How easy or difficult do you find it to make plans with someone on Tinder? Do you ever experience frustration dealing with the logistics of the date?

Sometimes, I have a very busy schedule. Im reluctant to meet someone new if I have had a busy day because I don't want to be tired or a bore at the first meeting.

Q9

Which factors attribute most to the success or failure of a Tinder Date? Describe in as much or as little detail as you want. [Success does not necessarily mean sex, but more did the date end leaving you wanting to see that person again? If so, why?]

Great conversation is number 1. You can be all kinds of pretty but if you're dumb as dirt, it ain't gonna last. Be engaging, witty, open minded and be able to handle a witty conversation.

• • •

Q1

What city and country do you currently live in/most use Tinder in?

Wellington, NZ

Q2

I am a

Female

Q3

How often do you initiate conversations on Tinder?

Sometimes (~50% of the time)

Q4

If you do initiate, how does the conversation usually flow? If it doesn't lead to a date, where does the conversation usually dry up?

If conversation gets boring, no banter, or they don't seem interested

Q5

When you get messaged first: how does the conversation usually flow?

Respondent skipped this question

Q6

Do any conversations stand out more than others? If so, why? For better or worse. Ideally, I'm looking for conversations that stand out in a good way but feel free to write about a bad experience as well.

Witty banter is always a good thing! And asking questions about each other makes it flow better. Not delaying the 'date' too long either.

Q7

How often do conversations that stand out (in a good way) lead to a date?

Once in a while

Q8

How easy or difficult do you find it to make plans with someone on Tinder? Do you ever experience frustration dealing with the logistics of the date?

No not really

Q9

Which factors attribute most to the success or failure of a Tinder Date? Describe in as much or as little detail as you want. [Success does not necessarily mean sex, but more did the date end leaving you wanting to see that person again? If so, why?]

If there is a connection and you get along well. Tinder or no tinder, chemistry and connection are the most important part of dating

• • •

Q1

What city and country do you currently live in/most use Tinder in?

New Zealand

Q2

I am a

Female

Q3

How often do you initiate conversations on Tinder?

Sometimes (~50% of the time)

Q4

If you do initiate, how does the conversation usually flow? If it doesn't lead to a date, where does the conversation usually dry up?

Say a witty comment about a photo the person has on their profile.

If it doesn't lead to a date, conversation usually dries up if lots of back and forth chat and no mention of meeting up or no set meet up plans are made.

Q5

When you get messaged first: how does the conversation usually flow?

If they just say hey, I say hey back and usually common questions about what do you do etc.

If witty comment is made about a photo or comment about the info in bio usual banter, trying to be funny etc

Q6

Do any conversations stand out more than others? If so, why? For better or worse. Ideally, I'm looking for conversations that stand out in a good way but feel free to write about a bad experience as well.

Light hearted convos that don't ask all the usual boring questions about work and what you up to today.

People that ask to go on a date quickly rather than just all talk.

Worst convos are when boys say or suggest having sex - or try and sext. That's not my thing and it's a major turn off for wanting to meet them or

Continue to talk to them. If I wanted to randomly bang someone I'd do the usual one night stand met them drunk in a bar.

Q7

How often do conversations that stand out (in a good way) lead to a date?

Once in a while

Q8

How easy or difficult do you find it to make plans with someone on Tinder? Do you ever experience frustration dealing with the logistics of the date?

It's as easy or difficult as you make it. If you're into it you will make it happen

Q9

Which factors attribute most to the success or failure of a Tinder Date? Describe in as much or as little detail as you want. [Success does not necessarily mean sex, but more did the date end leaving you wanting to see that person again? If so, why?]

Success is when you feel like you've made a friend and want to see them again.

Failure is the opposite

• • •

Q1

What city and country do you currently live in/most use Tinder in?

Nashville, TN

Q2

I am a

Female

Q3

How often do you initiate conversations on Tinder?

Less Often (<50% of the time)

Q4

If you do initiate, how does the conversation usually flow? If it doesn't lead to a date, where does the conversation usually dry up?

When other party becomes too pushy or uncomfortable.

Q5

When you get messaged first: how does the conversation usually flow?

Respondent skipped this question

Q6

Do any conversations stand out more than others? If so, why? For better or worse. Ideally, I'm looking for conversations that stand out in a good way but feel free to write about a bad experience as well.

Good- when other party uses humor, is open to talking for entertainment rather than immediately meeting

Q7

How often do conversations that stand out (in a good way) lead to a date?

Sometimes

Q8

How easy or difficult do you find it to make plans with someone on Tinder? Do you ever experience frustration dealing with the logistics of the date?

Easy but not always wanted

Q9

Which factors attribute most to the success or failure of a Tinder Date? Describe in as much or as little detail as you want. [Success does not necessarily mean sex, but more did the date end leaving you wanting to see that person again? If so, why?]

Light and polite interaction

• • •

Q1

What city and country do you currently live in/most use Tinder in?

Australia

Q2

I am a

Female

Q3

How often do you initiate conversations on Tinder?

Never

Q4

If you do initiate, how does the conversation usually flow? If it doesn't lead to a date, where does the conversation usually dry up?

Respondent skipped this question

Q5

When you get messaged first: how does the conversation usually flow?

Mostly question and answers at first, if a mutual interest pops up that will be discussed. Rarely do I get messages that are pick up lines or ice breakers. I have a rule that if a guy can message for a full 48hours then I'll meet up with him, but mostly conversation dries up before then

Q6

Do any conversations stand out more than others? If so, why? For better or worse. Ideally, I'm looking for conversations that stand out in a good way but feel free to write about a bad experience as well.

Guys that use unusual questions or "Would you Rather" games tend to stick out because it's not the boring "How are you? What do you do" routine. Had a guy would played Truth or Dare, that was interesting and fun and leaves the more routine questions for your (hopefully) first date so your not stuck looking for things to talk about when you do meet in person.

Q7

How often do conversations that stand out (in a good way) lead to a date?

Once in a while

Q8

How easy or difficult do you find it to make plans with someone on Tinder? Do you ever experience frustration dealing with the logistics of the date?

Guys are keen to set up a date for the future, for example saying we should catch up next week. Then they never follow through. If I'm the one initiating the date I always follow with a confirmation message the day before I want to go on the date. I find that guys are more "here and now" on Tinder, because they can just keep swiping until they find someone who will go out with them straight away

Q9

Which factors attribute most to the success or failure of a Tinder Date? Describe in as much or as little detail as you want. [Success does not necessarily mean sex, but more did the date end leaving you wanting to see that person again? If so, why?]

My first ever Tinder date a year ago actually resulted in a 9month relationship. I'm back on Tinder now trying to recapture that initial excitement of having a person actually interested enough to follow through with a second date. Honestly about what you're looking for from your first date is vital. If you're just looking to hook up, I don't go for that, so if you're just putting in the minimum effort you're not going to succeed. A guy that is engaged with what you're saying, and can ask follow up questions and hold your attention is worth a second date.

• • •

Q1

What city and country do you currently live in/most use Tinder in?

Sydney

Q2

I am a

Female

Q3

How often do you initiate conversations on Tinder?

Never

Q4

If you do initiate, how does the conversation usually flow? If it doesn't lead to a date, where does the conversation usually dry up?

Respondent skipped this question

Q5

When you get messaged first: how does the conversation usually flow?

Short and sharp until something mutual comes up and then it flows more

Q6

Do any conversations stand out more than others? If so, why? For better or worse. Ideally, I'm looking for conversations that stand out in a good way but feel free to write about a bad experience as well.

Conversation with my current boyfriend whom I met on tinder - light hearted and funny conversation which quickly led to a date. Not much boring chit chat online

Q7

How often do conversations that stand out (in a good way) lead to a date?

Once in a while

Q8

How easy or difficult do you find it to make plans with someone on Tinder? Do you ever experience frustration dealing with the logistics of the date?

Yea kinda - a lot of guys want to pick you up or meet at your house which is too risky in my opinion

Q9

Which factors attribute most to the success or failure of a Tinder Date? Describe in as much or as little detail as you want. [Success does not necessarily mean sex, but more did the date end leaving you wanting to see that person again? If so, why?]

Ease of conversation, mutual interests, Humour and light hearted chat

• • •

Q1

What city and country do you currently live in/most use Tinder in?

Sydney

Q2

I am a

Female

Q3

How often do you initiate conversations on Tinder?

Sometimes (~50% of the time)

Q4

If you do initiate, how does the conversation usually flow? If it doesn't lead to a date, where does the conversation usually dry up?

Mixture of results. Sometimes no response, sometimes lots of messages. Dries up after a week or so if no date.

Q5

When you get messaged first: how does the conversation usually flow?

Depends on the message. If it's lame I don't reply. If it's good, conversation can flow.

Q6

Do any conversations stand out more than others? If so, why? For better or worse. Ideally, I'm looking for conversations that stand out in a good way but feel free to write about a bad experience as well.

Funny jokes, interesting questions about my photos. Not so good and comments about looks/beauty.

Q7

How often do conversations that stand out (in a good way) lead to a date?

Frequently

Q8

How easy or difficult do you find it to make plans with someone on Tinder? Do you ever experience frustration dealing with the logistics of the date?

Easy. But need to organise relatively quickly or else interest can be lost.

Q9

Which factors attribute most to the success or failure of a Tinder Date? Describe in as much or as little detail as you want. [Success does not necessarily mean sex, but more did the date end leaving you wanting to see that person again? If so, why?]

Flow of conversation, things in common, if the guy at least offers to pay

• • •

Q1

What city and country do you currently live in/most use Tinder in?

Sydney, Australia

Q2

I am a

Female

Q3

How often do you initiate conversations on Tinder?

Less Often (<50% of the time)

Q4

If you do initiate, how does the conversation usually flow? If it doesn't lead to a date, where does the conversation usually dry up?

Usually after a couple of get to know you back and forwards.

Q5

When you get messaged first: how does the conversation usually flow?

Its either excellent and the conversation flows. But generally it doesn't go anywhere after a hello. Often they will say how are you doing – I will reply and then they say nothing back.

Q6

Do any conversations stand out more than others? If so, why? For better or worse. Ideally, I'm looking for conversations that stand out in a good way but feel free to write about a bad experience as well.

A good conversation for me is someone who asks interesting and unique things not just 'What is your name short for'.

Q7

How often do conversations that stand out (in a good way) lead to a date?

Once in a while

Q8

How easy or difficult do you find it to make plans with someone on Tinder? Do you ever experience frustration dealing with the logistics of the date?

Logistics are never really an issue, when it comes to organising a date by then I would hope that we have exchanged numbers.

Q9

Which factors attribute most to the success or failure of a Tinder Date? Describe in as much or as little detail as you want. [Success does not necessarily mean sex, but more did the date end leaving you wanting to see that person again? If so, why?]

N/A - have yet to have a second date with a tinder person for various reasons.

• • •

Q1

What city and country do you currently live in/most use Tinder in?

New Zealand

Q2

I am a

Female

Q3

How often do you initiate conversations on Tinder?

More Often (>50% of the time)

Q4

If you do initiate, how does the conversation usually flow? If it doesn't lead to a date, where does the conversation usually dry up?

When someone goes complimentary/looks based/sexual instead of just talking like a human being

Q5

When you get messaged first: how does the conversation usually flow?

Depends how - if they start an actual good faith conversation about actual things it flows great. If they start sexual, looks based or thirsty I don't bother

Q6

Do any conversations stand out more than others? If so, why? For better or worse. Ideally, I'm looking for conversations that stand out in a good way but feel free to write about a bad experience as well.

Puns, jokes, natural conversation flow back and forth, questions and answers and both people volunteering information and contributing to the conversation

Q7

How often do conversations that stand out (in a good way) lead to a date?

Once in a while

Q8

How easy or difficult do you find it to make plans with someone on Tinder? Do you ever experience frustration dealing with the logistics of the date?

It's pretty easy - I'm in town, want coffee? And they say yes or no or no but make another plan

Q9

Which factors attribute most to the success or failure of a Tinder Date? Describe in as much or as little detail as you want. [Success does not necessarily mean sex, but more did the date end leaving you wanting to see that person again? If so, why?]

If conversation is as enjoyable in person (both contributing, both with interesting things to say, both giving a shit about what the other says, fun) then sure I'll hang with them again

• • •

Q1

What city and country do you currently live in/most use Tinder in?

Liverpool, England

Q2

I am a

Female

Q3

How often do you initiate conversations on Tinder?

Less Often (<50% of the time)

Q4

If you do initiate, how does the conversation usually flow? If it doesn't lead to a date, where does the conversation usually dry up?

Conversation usually starts with asking what does the other person do for a living/ in their spare time. Conversation usually ends when there's some mention of snapchat or meeting up to bang.

Q5

When you get messaged first: how does the conversation usually flow?

Depends on the person, I always reply if the conversation has started with something funny or relating to my profile. If the conversation has started with a simple 'hey' it usually doesn't progress

Q6

Do any conversations stand out more than others? If so, why? For better or worse. Ideally, I'm looking for conversations that stand out in a good way but feel free to write about a bad experience as well.

Conversations where people have something interesting to talk about always stand out. Talking about an experience they've had, places they've been and why they enjoyed it there, talking about hobbies or why they love/ hate their job. Generally someone you can hold a conversation with and not someone who blatantly wants to badly sext you and ask for 'naughty' pictures. Instant no go

Q7

How often do conversations that stand out (in a good way) lead to a date?

Once in a while

Q8

How easy or difficult do you find it to make plans with someone on Tinder? Do you ever experience frustration dealing with the logistics of the date?

Incredibly frustrating. Apparently living more than a mile away from someone means it's 'difficult' to meet with them. If they have a car there's usually a little more interest as it's easier for them to get around- I need to use public transport but that is not a problem for me. There's always plenty of talk about a date- where to go and what to do. But rarely ever does it happen, plus, I work most weekends so meeting at the weekend isn't normally an option.

Q9

Which factors attribute most to the success or failure of a Tinder Date? Describe in as much or as little detail as you want. [Success does not necessarily mean sex, but more did the date end leaving you wanting to see that person again? If so, why?]

Always love someone who is genuinely interesting- have I found many people like that? No. Sadly a lot of the boys I have met have very little to talk about, it's all about work or football (soccer), neither of which overly thrill me. A sense of humour is always key also, if you don't laugh at my shit jokes then sorry, I'm not game for spending more time with you.

Being a gentleman and listening is a winner for me, I like to talk a lot, so be prepared to listen and don't interrupt me. Also don't judge me on my past- I don't care what you have to say.

Failure to a date is someone who literally makes me want to fall asleep in the middle of them talking about the gym, or football, or how they usually don't go to this bar because it's full of tramps. Just don't. It's not cool guys

• • •

Q1

What city and country do you currently live in/most use Tinder in?

Wellington

Q2

I am a

Male

Q3

How often do you initiate conversations on Tinder?

More Often (>50% of the time)

Q4

If you do initiate, how does the conversation usually flow? If it doesn't lead to a date, where does the conversation usually dry up?

She stops replying/does not reply

Q5

When you get messaged first: how does the conversation usually flow?

Joke a bit, add context to our pics/bios, outline who we are

Q6

Do any conversations stand out more than others? If so, why? For better or worse. Ideally, I'm looking for conversations that stand out in a good way but feel free to write about a bad experience as well.

When the level of interest/engagement is equal

Q7

How often do conversations that stand out (in a good way) lead to a date?

Almost all the time

Q8

How easy or difficult do you find it to make plans with someone on Tinder? Do you ever experience frustration dealing with the logistics of the date?

A mix

Q9

Which factors attribute most to the success or failure of a Tinder Date? Describe in as much or as little detail as you want. [Success does not necessarily mean sex, but more did the date end leaving you wanting to see that person again? If so, why?]

Both of us are honest, clear, and conversation flows naturally

• • •

Q1

What city and country do you currently live in/most use Tinder in?

Philadelphia, PA, USA

Q2

I am a

Female

Q3

How often do you initiate conversations on Tinder?

Less Often (<50% of the time)

Q4

If you do initiate, how does the conversation usually flow? If it doesn't lead to a date, where does the conversation usually dry up?

The conversation will usually be a silly comment about one of the person's photos. There's somewhat of a tipping point, I think. Usually if the first five-ten message exchanges don't flow naturally, I'll stop responding. If past that, we'll usually meet up.

Q5

When you get messaged first: how does the conversation usually flow?

They usually begin with a question about bicycle touring or stand up comedy, since my pictures have me doing both. I'll tell 'em something witty and usually will ask about something broader like comedy shows or travel in general or their bike.

Q6

Do any conversations stand out more than others? If so, why? For better or worse. Ideally, I'm looking for conversations that

stand out in a good way but feel free to write about a bad experience as well.

Oh absolutely. Some people start with good questions, like "what was the point you thought you'd make it [across America by bike]?" or "What's the least terrible place to watch amateur comics in Philly?" Or another favorite is people asking me about the types of bikes I have. With guys who really know philly biking, we can definitely banter about our favorite trails and bikes fairly easily. Another especially good one was someone (who I actually just went on a great date with yesterday!)who asked me to tell him something personal that I wouldn't usually tell a stranger-- that conversation got intimate pretty quickly.

I never respond to simple "hey :)"s, and usually am turned off by an immediate suggestion to meet up.

Q7

How often do conversations that stand out (in a good way) lead to a date?

Almost all the time

Q8

How easy or difficult do you find it to make plans with someone on Tinder? Do you ever experience frustration dealing with the logistics of the date?

In Philly, so easy. The city is dense and the transit is good, so I can walk or bike or subway to dates really easily. Usually, he or I will message/text for maybe two-three days, and then one of us will suggest meeting up a few days later. I've never had someone not follow through.

In Miami (where I've also dated), it's a lot more difficult. I don't drive so usually have to ask to be picked up, which is a lot more effort on their part and involves me trusting the person enough to get in the car with them before meeting them. Also, if the date doesn't go well, then you're subjected into being in a car together for a while after.

Q9

Which factors attribute most to the success or failure of a Tinder Date? Describe in as much or as little detail as you want. [Success does not necessarily mean sex, but more did the date end leaving you wanting to see that person again? If so, why?]

Tinder definitely favors extroverts. Since I can usually tell if I want to see the person again within the first few minutes of our date, people who take longer to warm up are often written off prematurely.

Planning a nice date definitely helps. Something with two parts (dinner then a walk in a cool neighborhood, biking then cooking together, etc) shows that the person actually is interested in the date, not just a potential hook up.

I probably see about a third of the men I date a second time. The ones I do see again simply had a great personality click with mine.

• • •

Q1

What city and country do you currently live in/most use Tinder in?

United States

Q2

I am a

Female

Q3

How often do you initiate conversations on Tinder?

Sometimes (~50% of the time)

Q4

If you do initiate, how does the conversation usually flow? If it doesn't lead to a date, where does the conversation usually dry up?

Very awkward and/or too fast. Dries up after a few days.

Q5

When you get messaged first: how does the conversation usually flow?

Not well

Q6

Do any conversations stand out more than others? If so, why? For better or worse. Ideally, I'm looking for conversations that stand out in a good way but feel free to write about a bad experience as well.

The weirder ones and the bad ones. Sometimes the weird ones are less flirtatious but those are the most enjoyable. It's someone else who recognizes who vapid the app is and keeps it in perspective.

Q7

How often do conversations that stand out (in a good way) lead to a date?

Almost never

Q8

How easy or difficult do you find it to make plans with someone on Tinder? Do you ever experience frustration dealing with the logistics of the date?

Pretty easy, although still flaky and unreliable.

Q9

Which factors attribute most to the success or failure of a Tinder Date? Describe in as much or as little detail as you want. [Success does not necessarily mean sex, but more did the date end leaving you wanting to see that person again? If so, why?]

Legitimate connection that doesn't lead to sex = successful Tinder date.

• • •

Q1

What city and country do you currently live in/most use Tinder in?

Wellington, New Zealand

Q2

I am a

Female

Q3

How often do you initiate conversations on Tinder?

More Often (>50% of the time)

Q4

If you do initiate, how does the conversation usually flow? If it doesn't lead to a date, where does the conversation usually dry up?

If they talk straight away about sex. Nope. If they pull out sexism, racist, homophobic bullshit etc. Nope. If they talk in text lingo. Nope. If they can't hold a conversation for more than a couple of days. Nope.

Q5

When you get messaged first: how does the conversation usually flow?

Hi, HI, how's your day, good add story here, cool wanna fuck?, SILENCE.

Q6

Do any conversations stand out more than others? If so, why? For better or worse. Ideally, I'm looking for conversations that stand out in a good way but feel free to write about a bad experience as well.

Interesting questions and interacting with the answers. Remembering the answers later.

Q7

How often do conversations that stand out (in a good way) lead to a date?

Frequently

Q8

How easy or difficult do you find it to make plans with someone on Tinder? Do you ever experience frustration dealing with the logistics of the date?

Yes. But that's coz I'm busy with life and they're impatient. Which usually means it never happens

Q9

Which factors attribute most to the success or failure of a Tinder Date? Describe in as much or as little detail as you want. [Success does not necessarily mean sex, but more did the date end leaving you wanting to see that person again? If so, why?]

Honesty having been a factor in the initial conversation. Them remembering the conversation and using it to help talk in person.

• • •

Q1

What city and country do you currently live in/most use Tinder in?

Wellington

Q2

I am a

Female

Q3

How often do you initiate conversations on Tinder?

Less Often (<50% of the time)

Q4

If you do initiate, how does the conversation usually flow? If it doesn't lead to a date, where does the conversation usually dry up?

I don't normally initiate because I don't like making the effort, but if I do I would say 10% of the time it leads to a date, and then that date is successful about 50% of the time

Q5

When you get messaged first: how does the conversation usually flow?

As a straight girl, straight boys are generally infuriating and always say the same thing. SO PAINFULLY no one ever says anything other than hey what's up wanna send me sum picz?

Q6

Do any conversations stand out more than others? If so, why? For better or worse. Ideally, I'm looking for conversations that

stand out in a good way but feel free to write about a bad experience as well.

I like people who make jokes about your photos or your descriptions. I'm pretty weird so it's nice when people stand out in that way.

Q7

How often do conversations that stand out (in a good way) lead to a date?

Frequently

Q8

How easy or difficult do you find it to make plans with someone on Tinder? Do you ever experience frustration dealing with the logistics of the date?

I would generally give someone my number once we agree to go on a date and we organise stuff that way!

Q9

Which factors attribute most to the success or failure of a Tinder Date? Describe in as much or as little detail as you want. [Success does not necessarily mean sex, but more did the date end leaving you wanting to see that person again? If so, why?]

Getting laid. I guess not being awkward and feeling like you have a connection. I'm trying to move away from completely casual sex so I feel it's successful when someone holds your hand or kisses your cheek cause it feels more personal!

• • •

Q1

What city and country do you currently live in/most use Tinder in?

Wellington, New Zealand

Q2

I am a

Female

Q3

How often do you initiate conversations on Tinder?

Less Often (<50% of the time)

Q4

If you do initiate, how does the conversation usually flow? If it doesn't lead to a date, where does the conversation usually dry up?

Conversation usually flows fine, but men seem to assume you're desperate if you've sent them a message. This usually leads to bizarre requests.

Q5

When you get messaged first: how does the conversation usually flow?

Usually fine

Q6

Do any conversations stand out more than others? If so, why? For better or worse. Ideally, I'm looking for conversations that stand out in a good way but feel free to write about a bad experience as well.

Conversations that start how you would speak to a friend flow better. If men start asking breast size or weird sexual questions I usually don't respond.

Q7

How often do conversations that stand out (in a good way) lead to a date?

Sometimes

Q8

How easy or difficult do you find it to make plans with someone on Tinder? Do you ever experience frustration dealing with the logistics of the date?

Scheduling is difficult but usually it works out

Q9

Which factors attribute most to the success or failure of a Tinder Date? Describe in as much or as little detail as you want. [Success does not necessarily mean sex, but more did the date end leaving you wanting to see that person again? If so, why?]

How the person you're on a date with treats you. If they're nice and behave like a normal person it usually ends well.

• • •

Q1

What city and country do you currently live in/most use Tinder in?

Auckland, New Zealand.

Q2

I am a

Female

Q3

How often do you initiate conversations on Tinder?

Sometimes (~50% of the time)

Q4

If you do initiate, how does the conversation usually flow? If it doesn't lead to a date, where does the conversation usually dry up?

The beginning of my conversations tend to be extremely crass and strange, in the hopes that I may prompt an equally interesting response. More than 70 percent of the time, this results in my immediate disinterest on my part. There have been occasions however when my lack of self control has paid off.

Q5

When you get messaged first: how does the conversation usually flow?

As I swipe specifically for men on Tinder, they usually take an aspect of my bio and repeat it back to me. Like a parrot. This does not always work in their favor, as I am an extremely sarcastic human and tend to overplay my words. Very normal and lovely looking people tend to take what I say as the solid truth and I have to break the news to them that I am in fact not 7'4.

Q6

Do any conversations stand out more than others? If so, why? For better or worse. Ideally, I'm looking for conversations that stand out in a good way but feel free to write about a bad experience as well.

Every now and then, when the planets align and Zeus smiles down upon my lot, I match with humans who are as mentally ill as my self. This provides for superb banter. One specific conversation read:

Me: "Fuck your mum. I'm sorry. She's probably a lovely lady."

Them:"Well I spent 9 months in her, whats another 30 seconds ammarite? Oh. Self burn. Where the aloe vera at."

The bad experiences don't appear to be as memorable. Those who can draw out the core of my personality in an instant are the ones who I invest more of my time in.

Q7

How often do conversations that stand out (in a good way) lead to a date?

Sometimes

Q8

How easy or difficult do you find it to make plans with someone on Tinder? Do you ever experience frustration dealing with the logistics of the date?

Not exactly. Traveling through different cities create difficulties in this area, especially if you are only staying for a short period of time. There have been occasions where I have matched with ferociously brilliant individuals in strange towns, only to leave the next day..

Q9

Which factors attribute most to the success or failure of a Tinder Date? Describe in as much or as little detail as you want. [Success does not necessarily mean sex, but more did the date end leaving you wanting to see that person again? If so, why?]

How interesting the person is to myself. I am a lady who likes to pick at peoples brains, for better or for worse. I always push for a reaction in a social situation, whatever it may be. If someone can keep up with my mental dissection and respond accordingly then usually I am hooked.

• • •

Q1

What city and country do you currently live in/most use Tinder in?

Chicago, il, USA

Q2

I am a

Female

Q3

How often do you initiate conversations on Tinder?

Less Often (<50% of the time)

Q4

If you do initiate, how does the conversation usually flow? If it doesn't lead to a date, where does the conversation usually dry up?

My initiations usually produce more dates than if someone contacts me (I.e., I like the chase). Conversation usually dries up if we've chatted for over 2, 3 hours and no attempt has been made to meet up.

Q5

When you get messaged first: how does the conversation usually flow?

I'm much more formal, more guarded when approached.

Q6

Do any conversations stand out more than others? If so, why? For better or worse. Ideally, I'm looking for conversations that stand out in a good way but feel free to write about a bad experience as well.

What I've learned is that people LOVE to talk about themselves, online and off. It's nice when I'm made to feel like not only am I being asked about myself, but I'm receiving thoughtful or funny responses.

My favorite messages with people on tinder have included us doing some sort of bit.

Q7

How often do conversations that stand out (in a good way) lead to a date?

Almost all the time

Q8

How easy or difficult do you find it to make plans with someone on Tinder? Do you ever experience frustration dealing with the logistics of the date?

It's as easy as the person messaging makes it. What is most useful to me about tinder is that you don't have to invest a lot of time in someone- so it's easier to walk away instead of dealing with frustrations. I'd say if you're both straightforward people who don't play mind games or abide by old "dating rules" (like the 3 day wait after getting a number) then it's super easy.

Q9

Which factors attribute most to the success or failure of a Tinder Date? Describe in as much or as little detail as you want. [Success does not necessarily mean sex, but more did the date end leaving you wanting to see that person again? If so, why?]

How much personality someone shows in messaging is the biggest factor. Their profile may be more earnest but they may have something totally different in the way they communicate.

My most successful tinder date(s) were with a guy who was kind and straightforward and had an honest representation of himself on tinder. I messaged him, we talked briefly, then made plans- it was simple. He made it feel easy to get to know him.

• • •

Q1

What city and country do you currently live in/most use Tinder in?

Chicago

Q2

I am a

Female

Q3

How often do you initiate conversations on Tinder?

Never

Q4

If you do initiate, how does the conversation usually flow? If it doesn't lead to a date, where does the conversation usually dry up?

Respondent skipped this question

Q5

When you get messaged first: how does the conversation usually flow?

Some basic banter than fizzles out quickly.

Q6

Do any conversations stand out more than others? If so, why? For better or worse. Ideally, I'm looking for conversations that stand out in a good way but feel free to write about a bad experience as well.

Someone who shows an interest in what I do with my life. Not trying to get immediate ass or be crude.

Q7

How often do conversations that stand out (in a good way) lead to a date?

Almost never

Q8

How easy or difficult do you find it to make plans with someone on Tinder? Do you ever experience frustration dealing with the logistics of the date?

Yes - I lose interest before meeting up becomes realistic.

Q9

Which factors attribute most to the success or failure of a Tinder Date? Describe in as much or as little detail as you want. [Success does not necessarily mean sex, but more did the date end leaving you wanting to see that person again? If so, why?]

Too many options. It reinforces the idea that larger cities are just giant playgrounds for young people, and there's no real reason to seek something substantial or commit. There's just too many options out there. We see our options every day on the street. Tinder reminds us how disposable the gender of choice has become.

• • •

Q1

What city and country do you currently live in/most use Tinder in?

USA

Q2

I am a

Female

Q3

How often do you initiate conversations on Tinder?

Less Often (<50% of the time)

Q4

If you do initiate, how does the conversation usually flow? If it doesn't lead to a date, where does the conversation usually dry up?

If I do initiate the conversation usually flows more quickly than if the other person initiated. It does not usually lead to a date. The conversation dries up when they stop responding or we both run out of references. My initiations are usually reference based. It is hard!

Q5

When you get messaged first: how does the conversation usually flow?

Slower. I never know what to say when they ask me, "What's up?" I usually put off answering for awhile.

Q6

Do any conversations stand out more than others? If so, why? For better or worse. Ideally, I'm looking for conversations that

stand out in a good way but feel free to write about a bad experience as well.

Yes, because they were ones based on genuine interest in me and what I do as well as the things we have in common. These lead to successful dates. One that stands out the most was when a guy I ended up dating for around 6 months messaged me saying that he noticed I worked at an improv theater and that he was new in town and looking to get into comedy because did stand up back home. After he messaged me again saying he was sorry if the previous message sounded robotic and promised he wasn't a robot. This gave me a lot to work with and made me interested in him as well.

Q7

How often do conversations that stand out (in a good way) lead to a date?

Frequently

Q8

How easy or difficult do you find it to make plans with someone on Tinder? Do you ever experience frustration dealing with the logistics of the date?

A little difficult. It can be frustrating going back and forth trying to make the decisions of when where to meet up.

Q9

Which factors attribute most to the success or failure of a Tinder Date? Describe in as much or as little detail as you want. [Success does not necessarily mean sex, but more did the date end leaving you wanting to see that person again? If so, why?]

Easy flow of conversation. If it is as easy to talk to you in person as it was via messaging I consider that successful.

Made in the USA
San Bernardino,
CA